Vogt Ranch living room, Christmas 1938. L to R: Peter Martínez, his father Andrés, Mother, Aunt Dorothy, Patti, Jo Ann, me & Father.

Mother with Navajo
neighbors, 1918

Bailing Wire & Gamuza

❦

The True Story of a
Family Ranch Near
Ramah, New Mexico.

✠ 1905 - 1986 ✠

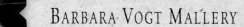

◄ BARBARA VOGT MALLERY ►

Dr. and Mrs Steinberg
with appreciation
of your interest
in my story.
Blessings,
Barbara Vogt Mallery
February 2004

Author: Barbara Vogt Mallery

Executive Editor: Bette Brodsky

Editor: Ree Strange Sheck

Book Design & Production: Bette Brodsky

Publisher: Ethel Hess

Library of Congress Control Number: 2003109632
ISBN: 0-937206-62-8

Printed in Korea

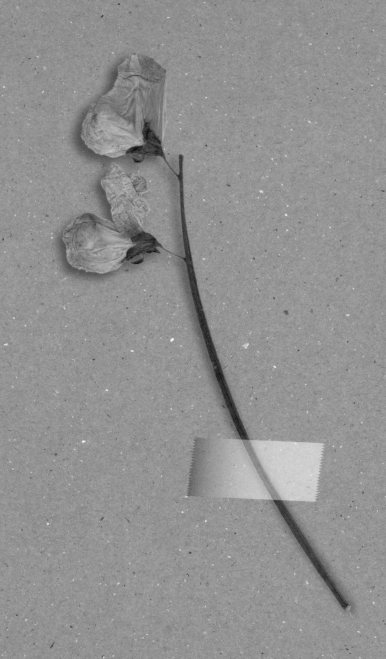

TABLE of CONTENTS

FOREWORD

Bailing *Wire and Gamuza* is a lovely memoir about a
special place and a special family in New Mexico. It
is gentle and insightful, deeply moving and often
quite humorous.

Barbara Mallery writes with lyricism and restraint
about good times, hard times and everything in
between. The Vogt family of Ramah built a beautiful
home with courage and tenacity, always hopeful
despite many setbacks.

This is a vivid and poignant little book, full of
shining culture and shining people. It is occasionally
heartbreaking, always heart-affirming. A special
addition to the history of New Mexico.

John Nichols
Taos, New Mexico
March 2002

Vogt Sheep Co.

Ramah, New Mexico

N⁰ 776

193___

PAY TO THE ORDER OF _____

FIRS

95-172

COMMERCIAL CLUB OF ALBUQUERQUE

OFFICERS

C. O. CUSHMAN · PRESIDENT
FRANK McKEE · FIRST VICE PRESIDENT
D. S. ROSENWALD · SECOND VICE PRESIDENT
JERRE HAGGARD · TREASURER
T. A. EGAN · SECRETARY

DIRECTORS

J. B. HERNDON   G. A. KASEMAN
FRANK McKEE   C. O. CUSHMAN
E. L. GROSE   D. S. ROSENWALD
JERRE HAGGARD   MAX NORDHAUS
J. T. McLAUGHLIN

ALBUQUERQUE, NEW MEXICO

Sunday
Oct. 11-14

Dearest Love Girl

Last night I got caught up in sleep.

I was out to a Carnival Party on the Street

Introduction

Working from my memories and from my father's files, I set out to write a memoir about the Vogt Ranch in an area of northwestern New Mexico where my father brought his bride in 1915 and where my brother and sisters and I were raised. The impetus sprang from the rich collection of photographs taken by my father, Evon Zartman Vogt, and the wealth of fascinating documents in his files, including journal entries and letters to family and friends, numerous letters written during the Depression and my mother's letters detailing her experiences with ranch life and her struggles during my father's absences.

I have tried to describe not only the natural beauty of the Vogt Ranch area but also the joy of growing up in a loving family. Our fun wasn't pegged to an abundance of toys. We often just used sticks and stones and sand and tin cans in our play. It was a rich time in a land steeped in history and cultures. Here our family of German-Swiss ancestry interacted with five distinct groups:

• the Mormon community of Ramah one mile away, where I attended school

• the Navajos, who were our closest neighbors

• the Zuni, whose pueblo was 25 miles away

• the Spanish-Americans from the villages of Tinaja, near the Zuni mountains, and Atarque, south of Ramah

• the Texans who settled near El Morro National Monument, 10 miles away, and also in the village of Fence Lake, 40 miles south, which they founded when they left the Dust Bowl during the drought of the 1930s

Many archaeologists and anthropologists visited and/or stayed with us as paying guests, enjoyed my mother's cooking and appreciated our information about nearby ruins and people for their studies.

City dwellers who slept late were a great concern to my mother, who was accustomed to fixing breakfast at the crack of dawn. I recall once when a guest came late for breakfast. My mother had tried to keep warm the many pancakes she had made for him and the early birds. The late guest commented that the pancakes would make excellent fly swatters if they only had handles!

I wish to acknowledge with much appreciation all those who had confidence in my writing ability and encouraged me to write this story: my sisters Jo Ann and Patti and my brother Vogtie, whose books were an inspiration. My gratitude also goes to my son Bruce who offered refinements to the manuscript; to my daughter Cathy and her husband Jim Ivanovich for their constant support and help throughout, especially on the computer; to my sister Patti who provided all the dates for the family tree; to my niece Anita Davis and her husband, Bob Schaefer, for corrections and suggestions; to Dorothy Perron, one of my first readers, who offered valuable guidance; to Mary Bergquist, who read the manuscript and made insightful suggestions and designed the family tree; to my friend Roberta Hanson, who was an important listener and critic as well as a computer helper; and to Colette Love, Jennifer Villenueve and Janice Scarpello, who put my writings on the computer.

Special appreciation goes to Bette Brodsky of *New Mexico Magazine* for her innovative book design and inumerable hours putting my story and photos together and to Ree Sheck for her efficient and creative editing. I especially thank John Nichols, whose favorable reaction gave me hope that my project could succeed.

Permission to use material has been granted by Geraldine Tietjen for historical information on Ramah, by Lisa Law for her photograph of my mother standing by the fireplace and by Nancy Dahl for her recent photograph of me.

Barbara Vogt Mallery
Santa Fe, New Mexico
May 2003

Mormon Boy Scouts
of Ramah, 1920

Father with Old Rafael, 1930

GAMUZA

"Gamuza" (gah-MOO-sah) is a Spanish word of Arabic origin for "deer hide" or "antelope hide." A tanned deer hide hung in the kitchen at the ranch, where strips of it could be cut off to use as shoelaces, or for a washer for a plumbing job, a spacer for woodworking projects or dozens of other necessities—sometimes a watch fob for my father.

◈※◈

Father in a tent house in Glorieta where he worked in the Glorieta Post Office & store, having left the University of Chicago due to tuberculosis, 1908

ailing wire and gamuza, humor and optimism, faith, love of family and friends and life in the Southwest, and pumpkin pie with whipped cream, all merged to help Evon Zartman Vogt, my father, through a lifetime of adversity. He, with my mother Shirley Bergman Vogt weathered snowstorms, drought, bad roads, financial problems, the death of a baby daughter and mother's periods of poor health.

My father's own battle with tuberculosis during his junior year at the University of Chicago brought him to New Mexico in 1906. During his recovery years he became fascinated with ranching as well as archaeology and anthropology. An uncommon ability to talk to everybody from scholars to sheepherders, his compassionate interest in the lives, joys and sorrows of others, and his constant journaling and photographing of these people and places, along

with letter writing, resulted in voluminous records of his life.

Dawn at the Vogt Ranch in northwestern New Mexico found him pounding on a portable typewriter with two middle fingers to describe his life to friends or to arrange business matters. Extensive files remain of his ranching activities as well as his El Morro National Monument custodianship; of campaigning for his friend Artie Bruce, who ran for governor of Tennessee; of scouting for gold mines in Nevada, Colorado and Mexico; and of his search for jobs during the Depression.

His correspondence reveals details of bailing a friend out of jail, building a dam, branding and earmarking sheep, investigating the possibility of raising goats to make cheese, transporting a Navajo friend to a health clinic, and taking in a troublesome teen-ager or relative of a friend in need of physical and/or emotional healing.

Immersing myself in my father's files, I found a letter written in 1910 from his ranch near San Mateo, N.M., to a college friend. This letter predates by five years his building my birthplace, the Vogt Ranch. He writes:

> The sun is just leaping over the peaks of the far-off Jémez Mountains. Across the great silent valley of grama [grass] and chamisa [a shrub] comes the fresh cool pure air of morning—so satisfying and healthful. For air and feed and view there may be better ranches but I doubt it. I am mighty happy in my little casita [house] all mudded now between the rocks and clean. Windows and doors and shutters painted green. But how much happier I would be if I could find a girl who could fit in here and be contented with the sky and plain, the timbered ridges, red mesas and wonderful mountains. One who could ride with me and be happy in the Great Solitude.

And he did find that girl "to fit in and be contented with the sky and plain." In fact, he met my mother Shirley after his brother Charles, older by 12 years, had married her widowed mother. As he visited during college years, he grew to love Shirley as she blossomed into maturity. They married in 1915 and moved to the Vogt Ranch, which is in the mesa and canyon country of northwestern New Mexico. It's a land of turquoise blue skies and whipped-cream clouds, of rust-and-buff striped sandstone canyons with dramatic weather-sculptured shapes silhouetted against the sky. This area is part of the Colorado Plateau, with piñon and cedar, ponderosa pine and oak trees, and firs and spruces at higher elevations. The ranch is 41 miles southeast of Gallup and 10 miles west of El Morro National Monument, where my father was the first custodian (see map on Page 34).

Evon Zartman Vogt was born on March 20, 1880, to Jacob Weimer Vogt and Magdalene Zartman Vogt in Upper Sundusky, Ohio. The Zartmans were residents of Württemberg, Germany, in 1700, and the Vogts lived some 150 miles south near Basel, Switzerland; however there is no evidence that the two families knew each other in Europe. The Zartmans immigrated to the New World in 1728, making the

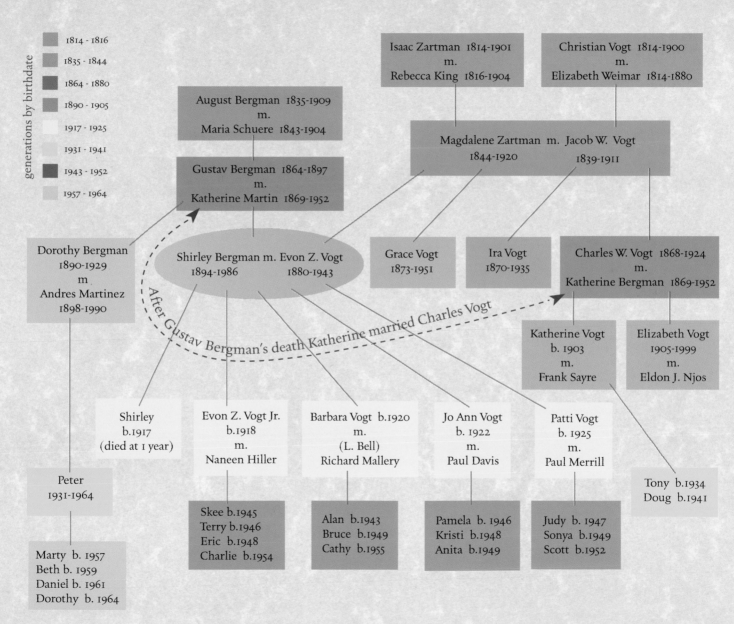

generations by birthdate

1814 - 1816
1835 - 1844
1864 - 1880
1890 - 1905
1917 - 1925
1931 - 1941
1943 - 1952
1957 - 1964

Isaac Zartman 1814-1901
m.
Rebecca King 1816-1904

Christian Vogt 1814-1900
m.
Elizabeth Weimar 1814-1880

August Bergman 1835-1909
m.
Maria Schuere 1843-1904

Magdalene Zartman m. Jacob W. Vogt
1844-1920   1839-1911

Gustav Bergman 1864-1897
m.
Katherine Martin 1869-1952

Dorothy Bergman
1890-1929
m.
Andres Martinez
1898-1990

Shirley Bergman m. Evon Z. Vogt
1894-1986   1880-1943

Grace Vogt
1873-1951

Ira Vogt
1870-1935

Charles W. Vogt 1868-1924
m.
Katherine Bergman 1869-1952

After Gustav Bergman's death Katherine married Charles Vogt

Katherine Vogt
b. 1903
m.
Frank Sayre

Elizabeth Vogt
1905-1999
m.
Eldon J. Njos

Shirley
b.1917
(died at 1 year)

Evon Z. Vogt Jr.
b.1918
m.
Naneen Hiller

Barbara Vogt b.1920
m.
(L. Bell)
Richard Mallery

Jo Ann Vogt
b. 1922
m.
Paul Davis

Patti Vogt
b. 1925
m.
Paul Merrill

Peter
1931-1964

Tony b.1934
Doug b.1941

Skee b.1945
Terry b.1946
Eric b.1948
Charlie b.1954

Alan b.1943
Bruce b.1949
Cathy b.1955

Pamela b. 1946
Kristi b.1948
Anita b.1949

Judy b. 1947
Sonya b.1949
Scott b.1952

Marty b. 1957
Beth b. 1959
Daniel b. 1961
Dorothy b. 1964

15

voyage from Rotterdam to Philadelphia and settling in Lancaster County, Pa. The Vogts made a similar voyage in 1750 and settled in what is now Union County, Pa. By the third generation, many Zartmans and Vogts had migrated to Ohio.

To give some flavor of my father's ancestry: the obituary for Christian Vogt, his grandfather who died in 1900, reports that he had 15 children, 37 grand-children and 22 great-grandchildren and that he had lived "a life of disappointment, bereavement, misfortune and sorrow, but God prospered him in his labors, enabling him to develop himself into a fine specimen of rugged manhood and to train up a useful and honorable family."

I reread my father's 1901 journal, written at age 21 in his senior year of high school in Dayton, Ohio, trying to get some insight into the major influences in his youth that might explain his exceptional strength in the face of adversity and his incredible optimism. He was a dreamer and a schemer who believed in the impossible (and my mother had the calm determination to make the best of it). The one thread that I noticed woven into his adult life was that of friend-

ship. This close association with friends that began with high school classmates is reflected in later years by his voluminous correspondence with fraternity brothers, historians, authors, anthropologists and archaeologists as well as family members.

The journal opens with his description of usher-ing in a new year and a new century. He comments on the changes in literature, art, ethics, theology, educa-tion and politics. He wonders, "Will the U.S. change its present form of government owing to its new policy of imperialism? What position will China play in the world's game of politics? Will aerial navigation be solved in this cycle of years? If so, what result will it have upon the life of man?"

It may have been typical of the times, but there seemed to be no casual hanging out or goofing off, although he does mention long visits with a certain Margaret and trying to get up the nerve to kiss her! On April 3, 1901, he wrote:

> I stopped at Margaret's for a few minutes. But I
> stayed longer than a few minutes. Indeed, I must
> have been there over an hour. She was seated in the
> big Morris chair and I was sitting on the arm of

the same by her, holding her hand, I believe.
Suddenly, the impulse seized me to kiss——yes, kiss
her. Before I knew it my lips touched her cheek. She
resented it gently and sighed as though struggling
with her will. . . . She said she supposed I had a
right to expect the privilege since she had said nothing
when I put my arm around her, still she hesitated
fearing that I would think less of her and saying
that she had already fallen enough from grace. I did
not believe she had fallen, nor that kissing her
would make me think a bit less of her, but rather, I
would like her better.

He also tells of taking a German class in the
evening and of his responsibility to check on the construction progress of his family home: on Oct. 14, he
wrote: "House is deserted today. Lathers left with
house half lathed. And plumbers didn't do a lick at
their work. I telephoned Mr. Myers and urged him to
whoop them up."

In a June 3 diary entry he refers to a sales job he
had with the county fair board. "Mr. Ferguson has
given me the privilege of getting out the Premium
Book, as last year, giving me 33% upon all ads solicited.
I am going to work hard and make my first money
independently in an honest way. If I get the same
amount of advertising I got last year, I'll make
$100.00."

He sold potatoes to a Cincinnati grocery with
classmate Herb Markham. Summer jobs after high
school graduation included salesman and manager of
collections for Book-Lovers' Library. On Nov. 3, he
wrote: "Mr. Hood [of Home Telephone] told me that
he had put me on the pay-roll for $60.00 beginning
November 1. This is $10.00 more for month that I
have been making and makes me feel decidedly better."

His early journal notations indicate a keenness for
marking history in the making. On Sept. 19, he
recorded:

Today the business of the country stops in a hushed
memory of our beloved president [William McKinley]
who lies cold, cold because of an anarchist dastard, at
his old home Canton, O. He will be laid under the
ground today. In every city in the land services are
going to be held according to President Roosevelt's
proclamation. At every train on most of the railroads,

streetcars, elevators and all will stop 10 minutes in order to express our reverence for the dead. All stores, all factorys are still and noiseless. All men are to go to their respective places of worship today at 2, the hour when McKinley's remains will be buried at Canton.

My father's New Year's resolution was "to be just." As he closed out a full year of journaling, his New Year's comments Dec. 31, 1901, were "I'll make no resolutions. Then I'll have none to break. I am going to try to control my passions better than I have, to stay home more nights, to be truer to my friends, to save more money, and to work harder."

In September 1902 he matriculated at the University of Chicago, having worked that summer in Chicago as a representative for the American League for Civic Improvement. In his freshman year he was on the freshman debate team. In 1903 he joined the Delta Upsilon fraternity and became an activist in fund raising for the fraternity by doing magic performances. In the summer of 1904 he worked for Scarborough Company Publishing in Indiana, selling newspaper and magazine subscriptions.

In his junior year my father was plagued with frequent sickness, finally diagnosed in the spring as having tuberculosis. Though he registered for the summer session of 1905, by fall he was advised to go to the Southwest for his health. Outpourings of concern about this news from relatives and friends are reflected in many letters that he kept.

Never in a sanitarium, he was treated for tuberculosis as an outpatient. He first lived and worked with the Eric Hunt family in Albuquerque in the Río Grande Valley of New Mexico. Staying in a tent in the orchard, he did chores in exchange for board. One of his letters explains: "This gives me outdoor air, sunshine, mind occupation, and decreases expenses. I get nine hours of sleep. Have gained five pounds."

From May to October 1906, my father worked for $25 per month for the Duncan MacGillivray sheep ranch in Estancia. Thus began not only his interest in sheep but also a friendship with this prominent New Mexico family. By December 1907 my father had relocated to the Pigeon Ranch in Glorieta, N.M., where he worked for William Tabor and his enterprises: farming, livestock and a general store.

From December 1908 to December 1909 he was involved in a Tabor-Vogt partnership, earning $50 per month managing the store and the post office. The old stone building that housed these businesses has been preserved to this day as the locale of New Mexico's Civil War Battle of Glorieta Pass.

During these Glorieta years my father was invited to join the weekend merriment held by prominent Albuquerque and Las Vegas families such as the Ilfelds and the MacMillans, who owned homes on the Pecos River near Cowles. The first time he went to one of these parties, he was not warmly welcomed as he was not wearing a tuxedo like the other men! He then sent to Chicago for his tux and would carry it on the back of his horse and change when he arrived at a party.

It is possible that some of the friends he made at these gatherings led him to the next venture, a 160-acre ranch in the San Mateo area near Mount Taylor. He went to work for the prominent rancher Floyd Lee and became half owner of the Merino Sheep Company with 3,453 head of sheep. His correspondence from this period—1909 to 1914—mentions his comfortable house and continued contact with Albuquerque friends, especially a relationship with a beautiful widow with two sons. One of these sons wrote my father in appreciation of his kindness and friendship. With his can-do approach my father solicited donations from college friends to buy a cupola and bell for the Mission School in San Mateo.

In 1914 he sold his ranch and his share of the sheep and used some of the money to travel in the United States and to Europe. Most importantly, he visited Shirley Bergman, with whom he fell in love. Her photograph rested on the mantel at his San Mateo ranch. He had watched her grow up and blossom into lovely womanhood during visits with his brother Charles (Shirley's stepfather) in Chicago.

While visiting family in Dayton, he wrote Shirley on May 28, 1914: "Your very sweet letter came when I needed it most—like rain after drought or roses after rain or kisses after fusses." He goes on to explain getting together with the old high school crowd and observes: "They all look sort of worried, sallow and hopeless in the eye. I hope nothing will ever take the sass and courage and vigor from my make-up."

Father with Floyd Lee, a prominent sheep rancher from San Mateo, NM, about 1910

FLOYD LEE

Floyd Lee (1895-1987) was the first man my Aunt Kay Vogt (Sayre) met when she moved to New Mexico after graduating from high school in Chicago. My father introduced her to Floyd at the Whitesides Cafe in Grants in 1922. Floyd had returned from service in the Army and was a cowboy on the 250,000-acre Fernandez Company Ranch northeast of Grants. A special friendship developed between Aunt Kay and Floyd, but she was not yet ready for marriage. Floyd later married Frances Marron. He eventually became the ranch's manager and by 1939 was the owner of the company.

Floyd was active in politics, serving 12 years as a state senator from Valencia County. For more than 30 years he was president of the New Mexico Wool Growers Association. Floyd was also known as the man who found and captured a wolf that later became the Lobo mascot for the University of New Mexico, according to his daughter-in-law Iona Lee.

Fraternity brother Buck Bukhauge convinced my father during a visit to Washington, D.C., that he should have the adventure of a boat trip to Europe and arrange to stay in Paris with Madame Pirolley, where Buck had stayed many years. So he booked passage on the U.S. Mail Steamship Co. *New York* ($55 to Cherbourg, France, by way of Plymouth, England) and sailed on July 17, 1914. "Mi Muy Querida Shirley [My Very Dear Shirley]," begins the daily journal of his boat trip, "so you will know what is going on with my life in the great alone." [Alone, with a crew of 451 and 700 passengers?] He describes the sea, the porpoises and the passengers lolling on the deck, games and races, a concert and a cabaret, even a suffragette parade with men dressed as women carrying hatchets and hammers.

He landed in Plymouth, England, crossed the English Channel to Cherbourg, then went on to Paris. When he became sick with a cold, Madame Pirolley rubbed his chest, gave him cough syrup, a nasal inhalant and "cupped" his chest with small wine glasses, creating suction by lighting cigarette papers in the glass, then inverting them quickly. When he did not improve, he went to the American Hospital, which was a former chateau with lovely gardens developed by Louis XV.

His frequent letters to Shirley described the intense atmosphere in Paris as World War I was declared, martial law was declared and universal mobilization began. "Every son, father, brother, and sweetheart aged 21-48 is being called to the frontier. Madame Pirolley continues to cry and worry, but cooks fine meals and is good to me."

Although the Paris he expected to see was no longer available, he did visit Versailles and the Louvre and took an intense interest in the mobilization process: soldiers parading, women replacing men as streetcar conductors, airplanes flying. When all foreign visitors were required to prove their nationality and get a permit to remain until transportation to leave was available, he waited in line four hours with 2,000 other foreigners. Presumably because of his German name, the French secret police searched his personal effects to make sure he was not a German spy!

One of the most heartwarming accounts in his letters was of the Place de la Concorde in Paris, at the

Strasbourg statue. After French troops had taken Alsace-Lorraine (which had been lost to Germany in 1872), the people tore the mourning cloth from the statue, climbed up and placed a French flag in the arms of the stone figure of a woman and tied an immense scarf of French colors about her neck.

Finally one man climbed up and stood on her arms so he could reach her face and kissed it! Twenty-five thousand Frenchmen sang "The Marseillaise." In order to get to London and arrange passage home, he slept across from the train depot and got up at 5 a.m. to get a seat. In London he joined the crush of thousands of Americans competing for information at the Savoy Hotel and for space on a ship. The rich were buying up available rooms for the crossing at fabulous prices. Finally he arranged to sail from Liverpool Aug. 19, and arrived in New York Harbor Aug. 30, 1914.

Mother, in center, with chums from high school, 1914

Glorieta Post Office & store with people involved in Tabor-Vogt partnership at Pigeon Ranch. (Father is second from right, 1908)

A group of our people in front of the store

Enriquez Rivera
Refugio Gutierez
Tom Bartlett
Lorenzo Sandoval
GLORIETA POST OFFICE STORE

Van Antonio Yleitt.
W. M. Tabor
Ezl. Lee Williams.

Father with lambs, San Mateo, NM, 1910

23

THE ALVARADO   FRED HARVEY   ALBUQUERQUE, N

Thanksgiving

Dearest You

I got in

walking up

ALVARADO.   FRED HARVEY   ALBUQUERQUE, N. M.

Miss Shirley Bergman
102 04 Seeley Ray
Chicago

Tied up with jute string—the kind used to stitch up gunnysacks—are many love letters from my father to my mother, an intense courtship by mail to which she responded with thoughtfulness and seriousness. In one letter he admits that seeing her upon his return from Europe in September 1941 overwhelmed him with the conviction that she was the one. The biweekly letters from wherever he was, describing his adventures as well as the constancy and depth of his love, proved this.

In October 1914, writing from the Commercial Club in Albuquerque where he lodged, received his mail, caught up on newspapers and visited friends, he responded to her letter about feeling blue by saying he was known as a dispenser of cheer but also had his own "down times."

On Sundays, instead of joining the poker or billiard crowd, he went to the sanitarium to visit friends with tuberculosis. One letter was written on the brown wrapper from a magazine he had in his saddlebag and described the hogan and simple possessions of his Navajo friend Tomás, whom he was visiting. After enjoying the mutton, tortilla and coffee they served him, he sat on a sheep pelt, writing to share it all with Shirley. A December 1914 letter inquires: "Can you make noodles and nut cake and be so interested in me that the bright lights won't call you more than the pines, the mountains and the stars? You must be sure."

He made a concentrated effort to find suitable land for his planned cattle business and for a home for the woman he wished to marry. A ranch near Las Vegas turned out to be all scenery and no good grazing, so he continued discussions with his friend

RAMAH

Settled in 1866 by Mormon missionaries to the Indians, the village of Ramah is in the foothills of the Zuni Mountains in northwest New Mexico. The homes and unpaved streets were shaded with Carolina poplars and Lombardy poplars, and irrigation ditches ran from Ramah Lake, which lies in a picturesque canyon. Ramah citizens were frugal. They canned the produce from their gardens or kept it in a root cellar, and huge beanbag chairs sometimes stored dried pinto beans!

WAR TIME CELEBRATIONS

During World War II many dances honored servicemen home on leave or missionaries going off for two-year assignments. The music of fiddle, guitar and honky-tonk piano wafted out into the night as the cowboy-hat-wearing "tejano" dancers wandered out to their cars to swig on their "salty dog"—grapefruit juice and tequila in pint jars. Rationing of sugar prompted signs in restaurants in nearby towns: "Use less sugar and stir like hell."

MODERNIZATION

Until Rural Electrification Administration power reached Ramah in 1948, most homes used kerosene lamps—the church had a gasoline-operated motor for electricity. Telephone lines came to Ramah homes in 1932, and in the 1940s, after many private wells ran dry, the town established a water system. The first television came in 1960.

HISTORICAL BUILDINGS

The Mormon church was the heart of the community. I recall the steeple of this church being adorned with an upside-down privy, placed there by some strong, imaginative and mischievous teenagers. On a luxuriantly shady corner was the Merrill Hotel (now the charming old two-story home of brother-in-law Paul Merrill and on the Register of National Historic Places) that accommodated teachers, telephone workers and anthropologists such as Clyde Kluckhohn.

FLOUR MILL

Davis Flour Mill, operated from 1934 to 1940 by Charles Davis, father of my brother-in-law Paul Davis, made flour, cracked wheat (called Charlie Mush) and corn meal.

THE RAMAH SCHOOL

During my high school years in Ramah, there were only 100 students in grades one through 12. Some of the teachers needed grammar lessons: I recall correcting my fourth-grade teacher who wrote on the blackboard that the contraction of "will not" was "willn't"!

Clark Carr; by January 1915 they had reached an agreement. Writing on letterhead from the Fred Harvey Alvarado Hotel in Albuquerque, my father describes the final deal: "I will become owner of 1/2 of 10,250 acres of land in return for three years' residence and services as manager of the property." He stated that the land near Ramah, N.M., was worth $15,000 at least, and in three years he expected to own cattle worth $5,000 to $10,000.

A three-year job may not have convinced some prospective brides, but my father so effectively interwove his romanticized descriptions of the country and how cozy and interesting and peaceful their life would be, and how desperately and how absolutely he loved her, that by February 1915 Shirley had accepted his proposal. There is a congratulatory letter to her from Artie Bruce, my father's closest University of Chicago friend, saying, "Evon is my dearest and best friend and

R. C. Master with Navajo customers at his Ramah Trading center - a general merchandise store & busy center for trading with the Navajos who brought wool, lambs & pinon nuts to exchange for groceries & dry goods, 1915

ANASAZI RUINS

Ruins on the Vogt Ranch property are the remains of Anasazi communities, built by people who moved here over a period of 100 years from the large villages in the Four Corners area of the Southwestern United States. Most archaeological research suggests that the Anasazi, now often referred to as the Ancient Ones, are ancestors of present-day Pueblo Indians.

The Vogt Ranch area ruins are thought to have been occupied between A.D. 1225 and 1275 during the Pueblo III archaeological period, characterized by building in open valleys and in rock shelters. Speculations about why these villages were abandoned include drought, climate changes involving a drop in temperature and shorter growing season for crops, disease, and attacks by Navajos and Apaches.

✄✈✄

Anasazi cliff dwellings on the Vogt Ranch property, 1920

merits the best of friendship and love as he is an American prince in every sense of the word. I think you are just the right girl for the comrade of my heart."

After returning to his San Mateo Ranch area to trade steers for heifers and sheep for cows and to round up and brand baby calves, my father went to Ramah to begin his new life. Ramah was one mile from his new land and house site.

He arranged to board with Bob Master, an Englishman, and his charming Scotch wife who owned the Ramah Trading Company store. He enjoyed their two meals a day, plus English-style tea at 4 o'clock, and read the newspapers they received from London and Glasgow.

Shirley did not seem discouraged by stories such as the one about the mail driver who, having had to abandon his buckboard because of deep snow, borrowed a saddle horse from a rancher so he could ride the borrowed horse and carry the heavy mailbags on his own horse.

On May 4, 1915, my father writes that he had started building their house. He explains that the adobes he had made got caught in a heavy storm before they dried and could not be used. Instead he decided to build with rock from the nearby ruins, which would "make our home warm and lovely."

A letter of May 6 explains that they needed lots of household things but suggests that all shopping could be done in one day in Chicago: dishes, tableware, tablecloths.

They use red and blue here. Red is very sensible for everyday on a ranch. . . . It will be a big jump for you to come from a country where you are known for what you have in the way of worldly goods and in the way of clothing to a place where there is absolutely no competition on such things. No one cares if one has cut glass, silver or a Paris gown.

Our life will be an easy one in which love and contentment will be the main pursuit—not much to do and I want to always keep it that way if I can.

Little did he know about their future!

Apparently Shirley expressed some reservations about their compatibility because of her lack of education beyond high school. He reassures her by saying,

MORMON DAY IN RAMAH

ARRIVAL OF MORMONS

The most enjoyable happening each summer was a visit to Ramah on Mormon Day, commemorating the arrival of the first Mormons to the Salt Lake Valley on July 24, 1847. In the 1940s, at the peak of its popularity, this celebration brought hundreds to Ramah from Grants, Bluewater, Fence Lake, El Morro, Zuni, Gallup and even St. Johns, Ariz. The Zunis and Navajos arrived in covered wagons, wearing ceremonial clothes and a profusion of jewelry—concho belts, squash blossom necklaces, turquoise bracelets and earrings. A parade reenacted the Brigham Young trek from Missouri to Utah. Rodeos included bareback bronc riding, roping, saddle changing relay races, wild-cow milking, foot races, tug-of-war, and ribbon roping, in which a man ropes a calf and his girlfriend comes out and ties a ribbon on the calf's tail.

CHICKEN PULL

The chicken pull or gallo contests were discontinued in 1942. An interesting example of changing times was the substitution of a bag of sand for a rooster buried in the sand with his head sticking out. "The "chicken" was buried near the chutes and the riders circled it at a dead run. (Someone was waiting nearby with a double lariat to whip any horse that slowed down too much.) Each rider swooped down to the ground and tried to pull the chicken out as he passed. It was dangerous to lean so far over, for the rider could fall or the saddle could turn. Many times riders missed the prize, but when someone got it, the race was on. The rider had to get to the other end of the field, circle a cedar tree, race back to the starting line and throw the chicken into the chutes. This was no easy feat, for all the other yelling riders were desperately trying to jerk it out of his grasp."*

SUPPER & DANCE

Both activity-filled days ended with abundant potluck suppers and a pioneer dance, the last waltz being "Home Sweet Home."

✁

*Quotation is from *RAMAH, A Documentary History 1930-1995*, by Dr. Geraldine Tietjin. Published by Family History Publishers, Bountiful, UT.

"You are so sweet and pure and good and sensible and capable that I am filled with gratitude and wonder at my luck." He anticipates with much joy sharing his thoughts and problems and decision making with her and in getting her advice about building the stable, where to put the chicken house, etc. He mentions having her ride with him each day. Then he speaks of peaceful evenings of reading and playing music on the Victrola and having dinner parties with friends. He is excessively optimistic about the anticipated rapid increase in value of his land and of his cattle, which he hoped would soon allow them to travel.

The last letter in his bundle is written on the train to the wedding in Chicago. He says, "Everything is in fair shape at Ramah. Furniture all there, lumber there, cows doing well, fencing progressing." He ends with "I love you and will soon be with you never to part."

Shirley Bergman was born in Freeport, Ill., in 1894 to parents from such prominent families that the elaborate, detailed newspaper account of their wedding filled 4 1/2 columns. I think some of the amusingly exaggerated wedding account reflects qualities Shirley shared with her mother. "Mrs. Bergman is a lady who can grace the kitchen as well as the parlor. The home over which she presides will be full of sunshine and happiness and dark shadows will never cross the threshold through any fault of hers."

Shirley's grandfather August Bergman Sr. was born in Germany and came to America in 1852, at age 16, with his widowed mother. He was a very industrious lad who helped with family income by working in brick making for eight years. Then he started a livery business "with buggies, hacks, and carriages of the latest style and the finest teams ever seen on the streets of Freeport." This business later included agricultural equipment. He served as street commissioner, alderman and then in 1885 as mayor.

Shirley's father Gus Bergman was described as having his father's rare business ability and pluck and was given half interest in the livery business. Tragically, Gus died at the age of 32 following a train accident, leaving two young daughters, Dorothy, age 6, and Shirley, age 3. They moved with their mother to Chicago to be with some of their mother's family.

While Shirley's mother was working at Marshall Fields in Chicago, she met my father's older brother, Charles, fell in love and married him. Various written records and memories provide information that they lived in three different rented homes before there was some money from the Bergman estate farm-implement business to build the home on Seeley Avenue where my parents were married in 1915.

Shirley's half-sister, Kay Sayre, a longtime resident of Santa Fe, now age 99, recalls the beautiful wedding bouquet the groom delivered the day before the wedding requesting that it be hidden as a surprise for the bride. So the bouquet of roses and lilies of the valley was hidden under a bed and peeked at frequently by the half-sisters, Kay and Betty. Kay remembers "crying buckets" when Shirley left on the train for her new life in New Mexico. Imagine growing up in the city of Chicago and then being taken on a honeymoon horseback pack trip in the Sangre de Cristo Mountains of New Mexico!

Mother & Father on their wedding day at Mother's home in Chicago on July 15, 1915

32

Father & Mother setting out on horseback for
their camping honeymoon in New Mexico, July
1915

Mother & Father - newlyweds at the Vogt Ranch, 1915

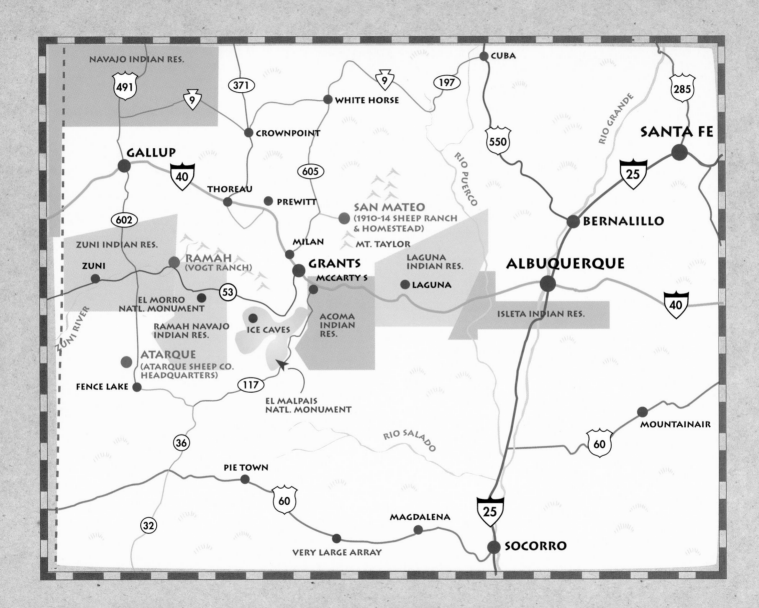

NAVAJO INDIAN RES.

491

9

371

9

197

CUBA

285

WHITE HORSE

CROWNPOINT

550

SANTA FE

GALLUP

40

25

605

THOREAU

PREWITT

BERNALILLO

602

SAN MATEO
(1910-14 SHEEP RANCH
& HOMESTEAD)

RIO PUERCO

RIO GRANDE

ZUNI INDIAN RES.

MILAN

MT. TAYLOR

ALBUQUERQUE

ZUNI

RAMAH
(VOGT RANCH)

GRANTS

MCCARTY S

LAGUNA
INDIAN RES.

53

EL MORRO
NATL. MONUMENT

LAGUNA

40

ZUNI RIVER

RAMAH NAVAJO
INDIAN RES.

ICE CAVES

ACOMA
INDIAN
RES.

ISLETA INDIAN RES.

ATARQUE
(ATARQUE SHEEP CO.
HEADQUARTERS)

FENCE LAKE

117

EL MALPAIS
NATL. MONUMENT

RIO SALADO

MOUNTAINAIR

36

60

32

PIE TOWN

60

MAGDALENA

25

VERY LARGE ARRAY

SOCORRO

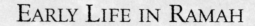

The honeymooners traveled by train to Lamy, N.M., 17 miles southeast of Santa Fe, and were met by a prearranged pack outfit—a packer-wrangler with riding horses and pack horses for the two tents, chuck boxes and supplies—to take them into the Sangre de Cristo Mountains. Even though it was mid-July, my mother recalled that at times the horses were walking over 20 feet of frozen snow, a perfect guarantee for coziness in a tent!

After the honeymoon, they returned to Lamy to catch the train, stopping to pick up crates of wedding gifts and household equipment stored in Albuquerque and then continuing West to deboard at Perea, just east of Gallup. From there it was by wagon to a sawmill camp in the Zuni Mountains, then on to Ramah by mail-carrier wagon.

My mother's description of this long, bumpy journey includes the incredible beauty of moonlit red-and-buff striped cliffs of the canyon they went through alongside moonlit Ramah Lake. When they reached Ramah, even though it was only a mile further to their new home—the Vogt Ranch—the driver said the horses were too tired to complete the trip. The bride and groom slept on the floor of the driver's home with family quilts and bedding so smelly with baby "tinkle" that my mother said she wished they had walked that last mile!

Among the treasures, once they arrived at their new home, was the Kalamazoo wood stove my father had purchased in Albuquerque en route to the wedding, which had been shipped to the ranch and installed, stovepipe, damper and all. Some 88 years later, it is still there.

One of my mother's immediate challenges at

the ranch was getting to know all the friends who came by. She was very frightened when a Navajo neighbor tugged at the locked screen door, exclaiming, "*Mucho amigo, mucho amigo!*". Not yet understanding Spanish, my mother did not know he was saying he was a good friend so she did not let him in. When my father returned, he explained that doors were not locked like in Chicago and that this was his good friend and worker from up the canyon.

And so life unfolded. In those early years, kerosene lamps provided lighting. Water was hauled up from the well by bucket. Sometimes bath water came from snow melted on the wood stove in an old-fashioned washtub. A wooden rain barrel just outside the kitchen door caught runoff from the roof, handy for hair washing and dishwashing. Clothes washing was done by hand, using a washboard and a bar of good old Fels Naphtha soap. Clotheslines were strung between piñon and cedar trees in the yard.

The original house was enlarged over the years. In 1916 a small screened porch was added to the front of the house; in 1917, a second bedroom, with a kiva fireplace in the corner. The present large kitchen was added in 1919, and then the partition between the original living room and kitchen was removed to form the existing spacious living room.

By 1922 a Delco motor with batteries furnished electricity, and a windmill with an auxiliary pump provided running water in the house. The most exciting modernization came in 1927: a bathroom with bathtub and washbasin. It was 1948, however, before we had a flush toilet. Finally, no more trips to the privy way out on the other side of the chicken house!

An adorable baby girl, Shirley Ann, was born in March 1917. Tragically, she died when she was 1 year old from spinal meningitis, thought to have been contracted during a train trip to Chicago. She was buried nearby in what is known as Shirley Ann's Canyon. Joy at the arrival of Evon Zartman Vogt Jr., called Vogtie, in August 1918 somewhat tempered the sorrow of Shirley Ann's death.

In 1920 when my birth was imminent, my grandmother Kate Martin Bergman Vogt came out from Chicago. When Mother went into labor, Grandma had to hike nearly a mile—over an arroyo and across the valley—to a Navajo hogan to ask the neighbor to

The boxcar that brought
the honeymooners from
Glorieta to Perea, NM.
Mother is on the right in
the open doorway of the
boxcar, 1915.

The original ranch house
was built in 1915 of
rocks taken from ruins
on the property. In 1916,
a small screened porch
was added.

Mother's half sisters Kay &
Betty, 1915

Mother holding Shirley Ann,
born in 1917

saddle up and go after my father at sheep camp. My father fetched a midwife from Ramah, who brought me forth alive, after removing the strangling umbilical cord from around my neck.

When my aunts Katherine and Elizabeth (Kay and Betty) graduated from high school in Chicago, their father Charles Vogt (my father's brother), who had lost his job at Marshall Fields Department Store in Chicago, moved the family to Albuquerque, joining his wife Kate, who had stayed to help Mother after I was born. So they were all in New Mexico in 1922 when my sister Jo Ann was born at the ranch. Jo Ann's special birth story is that the mattress on the bed was too soft and saggy for "good birthing work," so the doctor had the closet door taken off the hinges and put under the mattress to firm it up.

In spite of my father's valiant efforts to help his brother by involving him in the excitement of ranch life and the sheep business, Charles committed suicide in 1924 at his home in Albuquerque. My father, whom Kay and Betty called Uncle Evon, became a strong part of their lives. He enthusiastically exposed them to the adventures of life in the West. He took them to dances, taught them how to ride horseback, and took them to sheep camp. (Aunt Kay recalls that my father one time stopped by the side of the road outside Grants so they could change from blue jeans to dresses in order to be properly attired for the dance that night.) Since they had bobbed their hair in keeping with the 1920s trend, they took their curling iron along to camp and heated it in the coals of the campfire in order to marcel their bobbed hair. When my mother bobbed her hair, my father carried out the threat he had made—to shave his head if she ever cut her lovely long hair.

When the cattle business did not thrive as anticipated, sheep ranching became the main focus, with the new challenges of buying ewes and bucks, selling lambs for meat, and shearing seasonally for the wool market. One news article tells of father's purchase of 3,000 sheep that he paid herders to move from the Mount Taylor area to the grazing land near the Vogt Ranch—a trip that took more than a month. My father became very knowledgeable about where he could find herders, both Navajo and Spanish-American, about who would make the best sheep-camp cooks, when to move the herds to new grazing land, and how to arrange for dipping the sheep in a trough of Black Leaf 40 solution to control a disease called scab. He also learned how to perform castration on male lambs in order to improve their meat quality for market. He took great pride in knowing this process: the bottom of the scrotal sack was cut and testicles removed with the teeth, while the lamb's four legs were held by another herder. Using the teeth was considered safer for the lambs than using a sterilized tool.

In 1921 one of my father's contacts led to a job with Burgess and Spencer, which necessitated the family's moving to Glendale, Calif. In the correspondence Burgess and Spencer appeared to be brokers from whom my father bought lambs, placing them with grazing ranchers such as Silvestre Mirabal of San Mateo until they were ready for market. The deal did not work out. My father received no money. The family suffered through the flu epidemic while in California, and when we returned to the Vogt Ranch, we found all the Navajo rugs that had charmingly decorated our home had been stolen.

Never one to despair, my father returned to his own sheep business. Bank records and correspondence about land leases and bank loans reveal various sheep companies: the Ramah Sheep Company in 1926-27, the Vogt Sheep Company in 1927 and eventually the Atarque Sheep Company, organized and incorporated with investments from special friends Artie Bruce, Ray Smith (of the A. O. Smith Corporation), Bill Wrather (director of the U.S. Geological Survey) and Louis Dent, theater owner from Dallas, Texas. The Atarque Sheep Company leased several sections of land near the Spanish-American village of Atarque, N.M., 45 miles south of Ramah, and ran 12,000 head of sheep, with supply headquarters in the village.

One of the special times of my childhood was visiting my Aunt Dorothy in Atarque. My father had sent an SOS to Mother's sister Dorothy to come to the ranch and help out when the eczema on Mother's hands, a chronic condition since her youth, reached a crisis. By the time my siblings and I required less care and my mother's eczema was under control, Aunt Dor decided not to return to Chicago, where she had been studying at the Chicago Art Institute. She valued the freedom to wear bib overalls and arrange her braided hair in little buns over her ears. Because of her unconventional dress and hairstyle, we now think of Aunt Dor as the family "hippie."

She accepted the job of postmistress and storekeeper at the headquarters of the Atarque Sheep Company, imaginatively creating a small apartment in the back of the town's only store. I remember the dressing table she made out of two apple crates with a board across the tops. A pleated skirt hid the shelves she made in the crates and added a feminine touch.

A huge, long shed for shearing sheep was nearby, with its motor-driven shears. One day while I was visiting, Aunt Dor gave me a gallon jug of lemonade and asked me to take it to that handsome shearer in the shed, second from the end of the line of workers. This was Andrés Aragón Martínez, who became her husband. They eventually settled in Taos. Aunt Dor died in 1973; Andrés lived another 17 years. He married again—with a lifelong friend, Jeanette—and fought actively for the preservation of the acequias, or irrigation ditches, with their friend John Nichols, well-known author and conservationist of Taos.

Because income from the sheep was seasonal and

Mother on the left, wearing her honeymoon boots, her half sister Betty in the middle & her sister Dorothy on the right. Aunt Dor was the family "hippie." They are at the Atarque Sheep Ranch headquarters, 1931.

slow, my father sought other earning activities. Because of his fascination with and knowledge of El Morro National Monument, only 10 miles from the ranch, he became its first custodian, part time, in 1917 and served until 1920 at a nominal salary of $3 per month. In 1922 he was reappointed at $30.40 per month.

El Morro is a buff-colored sandstone monolith about 230 feet high. Carved on its walls are inscriptions by different parties that camped at El Morro dating from 1605 with the inscription of Juan de Oñate, the Spanish colonizer, and including conquistadors, priests, wagon-train travelers and Army personnel who camped at El Morro. These inscriptions were called "autographs in stone" by Charles F. Lummis, journalist, poet, editor and appreciator of Southwest peoples and places.

It was always a special treat to me to be with my father as he guided visitors around the base of the stunning sandstone bluff, pointing out Indian petroglyphs, reading aloud and then translating the Spanish inscriptions, explaining their ties to Southwest history. He also pointed out the Anglo immigrant names and the notable inscription by Lt. J. H. Simpson and artist Richard Kern of the Army Corps of Topographical Engineers, who spent two days copying the inscriptions in 1849. I recall his stopping at the permanent water hole in the cliff's cove to explain that this was the reason El Morro had been a well-used camping place between Acoma and Zuni pueblos. Then we would make the trip over the top of El Morro, always marveling at the sensational views, and once again he would explain that those notches in the Zuni Mountains across the valley were where dinosaurs had taken bites out of the mountain!

In 1925 my father worked for the University of Chicago fund drive, taking leave of absence from the National Park Service. For $74 per week plus expenses, he made appointments with prominent, wealthy alumni, scheduling them to speak at fund-raising events. In spite of the intensity of this job, the family took time out to celebrate my parents' 10th wedding anniversary with a return visit to the honeymoon spot on the Upper Pecos River in the Sangre de Cristo Mountains. And that same year, on Sept. 15, 1925, another baby was welcomed, my sister Patricia Pah

(Patti). In Navajo pah means "beautiful."

My father's enthusiasm and congeniality, as well as his need for income, led his fraternity brother Arthur Bruce to ask him to help with his campaign for governor of Tennessee in 1926. Artie did not win even though my father gave the campaign his characteristic dedication and determination.

During the Winter of the Big Snow in 1931 the tragic loss of cattle and sheep formed indelible memories. One in particular is of November when 3 to 4 feet of snow fell in 48 hours of continuous storm. Many Navajos were stranded while out picking piñons, and despite an attempt to move sheep down to available grazing land in Arizona, my father suffered considerable losses. That combined with the low market prices during Depression years resulted in my father's phasing out of the sheep business.

Moving the sheep to grazing in Arizona to try & save their lives during the Winter of the Big Snow in 1931

SHEEP IN NEW MEXICO

MAJOR INDUSTRY

Sheep raising was a major industry in New Mexico. According to a "Geographic News Bulletin" of Feb. 9, 1934, the state produced about a quarter of total U.S. production in 1932. But by the late 1980s, foreign competition, especially from Australia and New Zealand, along with increased labor costs, the federal government ban on Compound 1080 used to poison predators, and the trend toward synthetic and blended fabrics had decreased the market.

THREATS TO THE HERD

Coyotes were considered a major factor in dwindling sheep flocks. But sheep ranchers also were concerned about overgrazing and damage to the range by herds of wild horses and burros. Ranchers planted shelterbelts of willow, tamarisk, mesquite and cottonwoods to protect their ranges.

RAILROAD

By 1934 railways expedited moving sheep for ranchers who bought from neighboring ranches or livestock shows, but trucks hauling sheep could go only as far as passable roads permitted. Then sheep were unloaded and herded into the mountains for summer grazing or allowed to graze through mesa and canyon country untouched by roads.

CARING FOR SHEEP

The business involved buying ewes and rams, lambing, ear marking and castrating males (to produce better meat), dipping to treat scab, shearing, arranging for grazing lands, providing extra feed (barley and oats) when fattening for market. In drought years my father placed salt blocks on the range or added rock salt to the barley and oats and supplemented feed with calcium phosphate to improve lamb crop and fleece quality.

SHEARING

An article written in 1935 by my father explains that young rams—not more than 18 months of age—give the best service. Care should be taken to choose rams that are "strong, rugged, alert and courageous looking, showing a tendency to fight. Besides age, health and vigor, rams should be chosen also for underbody perfection—no damage from shearing to the working parts."

Father selecting rams in Arizona. L to R, Tom Hudspeth, E.L. Moulton, Father, 1935

Corner of an envelope from Vogt Sheep Company stationary

Sometimes passengers had to get out & push, 1920

Father bringing water from an arroyo for the boiling radiator of his Model T Ford

Lying under his bogged-down truck in the muddy road, trying to put chains on the rear wheels, my father exclaimed, "I'd like to get the guy who invented these chains and tie a rock around his neck and throw him in the Rio Grande!" It was about 1929. As always, he was trying to deal with adversity through humor. This outburst revealed his utter frustration over road conditions in the Southwest, particularly in his area of New Mexico. Getting roads improved became a major crusade for him since being stuck in the mud or snow demanded incredible time and energy.

I can remember spending eight hours to complete a 40-mile trip from Gallup to the Vogt Ranch. Getting unstuck was a challenge: gathering rocks and small branches and whatever brush was at hand to create traction for the tires, then unloading all passengers both to lighten the load and to have them push. It was important to know how to rev up the motor and "gun it" across an arroyo after a cloudburst.

One time my father had to give up on reaching his destination for that day because it was getting dark and he was too tired and hungry to continue. He unloaded his bedroll and made camp. While he built a fire, he happily remembered that there was a can of Campbell's Pork & Beans under the seat of his pickup that had been banging around with the usual tools carried by a Westerner. He eagerly opened the can—its label had been worn off by the tools—only to discover that it was a can of roofing tar!

My father's correspondence includes a letter to President Franklin Delano Roosevelt in August

GALLUP, NEW MEXICO

Originating as a stop on the A&R Railroad in 1881, Gallup takes its name from railroad paymaster David Gallup.

A MIXED POPULATION

The population grew with the Europeans, Asians, Mexicans and Anglos who came to work in the coal mines and on the railroad. Many of those families' descendants are still in Gallup; bearing such beautiful names as Radosevich, Landavazo, Miyamura and Ferrari.

INDIAN CAPITAL

Gallup became known as the Indian Capital of the World, partly because of the Inter-Tribal Indian Ceremonial, started in 1922, to increase appreciation of Indian culture and crafts. The first ceremonial exhibited crafts in tents. Spectators sat in their automobiles, with their lights illuminating evening performances by costumed dancers. By 1939 the ceremonial, in which 30 tribes were represented, had a special arena, with a grandstand for people who came from all over the world plus a large exhibit hall for the crafts. My father was on the board of directors of the Ceremonial Association as well as being the announcer at ceremonial performances. My mother made Navajo costumes for all four of her children to wear when we attended the performances.

GROWTH OF TOURISM

As the popularity of Southwestern jewelry exploded, tourism in Gallup enlivened the economy. Route 66 and parallel streets in Gallup came alive with shops offering Indian jewelry and Navajo rugs. Large mercantiles like Cotton's and Kirk Brothers shipped Indian crafts all over the world as well as to trading posts throughout the Southwest. Across the railroad tracks, warehouses stored wool in 100-pound sacks awaiting shipment to eastern woolen mills. Danoff's, a dry goods store, had Levis, velveteens and calicos for tourists and residents wearing the Navajo traditional attire. Gurley Motor helped make Gallup the "pickup capital of the world." Bubany Lumber, Gallup's "Home Depot," advertised roofing repair as well as lumber and hardware for shoppers from near and far.

1935 imploring him to help with road conditions. He described them as horrible goat trails that prevented homesteaders from Texas and Oklahoma from getting their crops to market, interfered with visitors to El Morro National Monument and wore out the cars of the U.S. Forest Service, the Indian Service, the Soil Erosion Service and the Department of Commerce. These cars, he wrote, "get bogged down, delayed, broken, and worn out in three months' service." He referred to John Collier, commissioner of Indian Affairs, who had painfully traveled these roads recently, and to Horace Albright of the National Park Service, who spent the night stuck in a bog with his family trying to get to El Morro. He pointed out that the Navajos in the area were almost as remote from school, doctor and market as people in the interior of Ethiopia!

So day after day, week after week, my father was

A photo of the parade during the Inter-Tribal Indian ceremonial in Gallup, 1922

Museum of New Mexico Archives
Photo by J.R. Willis
neg. # 134841

up at the crack of dawn pounding his typewriter since "somebody has to take the bull by the horns" and get the job done. Many urgent letters dealt with bureaucratic regulations. Also in my father's file are speeches to the Gallup Chamber of Commerce and articles and editorials from Gallup and Grants newspapers.

After the Ramah to El Morro road was finished, the equipment was used to scrape the road to Atarque, 25 miles to the south. The following account from my father's National Park Service report in April 1934 is quoted from a retrospective by Ted Rushton that appeared in the June 20, 1995, *Gallup Independent.*

> After finishing this piece of road we managed to get the use of the grading outfit for work to the southwest and financing it through Indian Service help, private donations and $300 from Valencia County. We flat-bladed a road 25 miles southwest to Atarque on which the culverts, hauled through the kindness of the Forest Service, are now being placed. It was a lot of fun staking out this road through the close timbered country to Atarque, which was founded by the first Spanish settlers in 1882 but which never has had anything but two high-centered, groan-producing ruts leading to it. The people at those Mexican ranches 20 and 25 miles from El Morro were almost alarmed at the great size and noise of the caterpillar as it dug into the dirt and made road as it went. At Pinitos where there is a 10-kid school, all Spanish, the teacher and all the children, boys and girls, followed us along for several miles to watch the work and once when the tractor stopped to be cooled off by a drink of water, they asked to ride. So we gave them all a chance to ride the vibrating monster. I offered to take them back in my car but they gladly walked to their poor little adobe school, greatly delighted with their wonderful experience.
>
> At Atarque the advent of the machinery was like a circus coming to town. Everything stopped. All four rooms of the school dismissed. One man came ahead on horseback to tell us that the women of the town were getting up a fiesta dinner for us while the rest of the village waited at the foot of the hill to see how the machinery would push the rocks and dirt away. The meal those good women got up for my greasy crew of

cat and blade men and three axe men who went ahead of us to help make clearing was an achievement which will live long in the crevices of my memory. Really, those inpanadas [correctly spelled empanadas, "a stuffed pastry"], chile con carne [made from hand-kneaded chile pods], the huevos fritos [fried eggs], not to mention three cakes and four kinds of pudding almost wrecked the outfit. The Mexican women assembled and served this food at one house and stood by to see that we did our darndest. That night they gave us a dance and we swung the señoritas until midnight.

The following news clip, dated May 1934 (source not given) reflects how my father did "take the bull by the horns" to solve the problem of the roads.

E. Z. Vogt, custodian of El Morro National Monument, deserves a great deal of credit for the work he has done in securing improvements for the highway from Gallup to Zuni, Ramah and Inscription Rock. After spending three days with G. D. Macy, New Mexico Highway engineer, Vogt secured $1000 for the road. Finding this insufficient to do the work as he felt it should be done, he called on Superintendent S. F. Stacher, Eastern Navajo Agency, to contribute $500 in Navajo labor; talked a Department of Commerce man into furnishing some cement and $175 worth of gas and oil; secured a promise from Superintendent G. A. Trotter, Zuni jurisdiction, to grade and drain the road and fix the bridges on the reservation; and borrowed a Caterpillar-60 from McKinley county. He even promoted a quantity of heavy spikes in Gallup.

With this money and cooperation he has bladed off the road from Gallup to Ramah, has started building a grade on a straightened course from the Department of Commerce landing field near El Morro to the line of the state survey made last year. After finishing these jobs Vogt will move the equipment to the northern boundary of the Zuni Reservation where he will spend two weeks grading up the road from there to Gallup and installing the 20 metal culverts that have laid beside the road for three years.

Playing house with dolls -
brother Vogtie stopped
teasing long enough to
pose for a photo
Patti on left, me center,
Jo Ann on the right, 1930

Ready for the one-mile
walk to Ramah school
From left - Vogtie, Me,
JoAnn, Patti, 1931

My parents' cheerful dispositions and firm, friendly discipline gave us a happy childhood with a balance of work and play. Hours were spent on games of kick-the-can, allez, allez, oxenfree and jacks. I recall in particular how we carefully layered sand of different colors in a jar to create scenes—the sand from rocks pulverized with a hammer. We took our dolls on camping trips back on the mesa, traveling with a little red wagon, using blanket-and-tarp bedrolls, just like the one my father took to sheep camp. We would make camp every few minutes as we traveled into the woods and prepare pretend meals from natural materials—juniper berries for peas, long seedpods from bee weed for green beans. Sometimes we made an outdoor home for the dolls, outlining the rooms with rocks from the yard. When we had to play inside because of the weather, we had permission to use books to build furniture for the dolls. We also played with string-wound tops and button buzzers made with huge buttons and string. With Vogtie we made stilts—tin cans nailed to pieces of wood— held on our feet with attached ropes, pulled up taut with each step so that the cans stayed against the bottoms of our feet.

We explored the woods and climbed up and down the rock escarpment along the edge of the mesa. We had no sodas to take on these outings. Instead we made punch in a pint jar of water in which we soaked the cut-up rinds from our breakfast oranges.

Years later, I delighted in watching my children enjoy an activity from my childhood: bumping down the rocky hill between the ranch house and the chicken house in the little red wagon. One day when they were taking turns with the child of a Navajo worker, my mother came out on the porch and called "Chineago hey!" Reminiscing at the end of our ranch visit, my daughter commented about the Navajo boy named Chineago Hey, whereupon I explained that this was Navajo for announcing a meal, not the little boy's name!

My memories of chores are happy ones, too: milking the cow, filling the wood boxes beside the stove and fireplace, gathering chips for starting fires, feeding orphan lambs with a baby bottle, helping cut blocks of ice from the frozen lake and canning fruits and vegetables. I washed dishes when I was so little that I had to stand on a wooden box that was used to store potatoes under the sink. I do not recall my mother ever scolding me for playing endlessly with the bubbles in the suds or watching water run through a funnel or a sieve while doing dishes. However, I *was* scolded if I let the water run down the drain instead of throwing it out on the petunias my mother was trying to grow by the porch.

By the time I was 14, I was very good at ironing with flat irons heated on the wood stove. It was like a game to choose the right iron for the garment. There was a large, a medium and a small iron. The big Daddy shirts were quicker to iron with the large iron. I remember one day there were 21 shirts: some white; most, faded blue-denim work shirts. The smallest iron was best for little girl dresses, especially if they had puffed sleeves.

Washday was a major undertaking. In earlier years laundry was done in a big round washtub with a washboard, all by hand, but later we had a Delco motor that generated electricity (before the Rural Electrification Administration reached our ranch). Starting the motor was the first step. Next the old Maytag wringer washing machine had to be rolled into position so that the electric cord would reach the outlet. Then the big washtub was fetched from where it hung on the side of the Delco house and placed on a stool alongside the washer. Both this tub for rinsing and the washer were filled from the sink faucets with a short hose. If we forgot to watch the water rising in the tub, it would run over. Or if we did not hold the hose, it would slip out of the tub and flood the kitchen.

We sorted dirty clothes on the kitchen floor into piles of washer loads—whites, light colors, dark colors, and blue jeans and work pants. I think there were usually seven loads, so the kitchen on washday was no place for a tea party. We renewed the wash water and the rinse water between loads by bailing out some water with a bucket and adding fresh water. The wringer through which clothes passed from wash to rinse had to be very carefully fed. For example, if a washcloth or napkin was fed by a corner, it would stick to the roller and wind up on it, which meant we had to stop and release pressure on the wringer to retrieve the cloth. Those buckles on the straps of bib overalls had to be folded into the large part of the garment to prevent sharp edges from cutting the wringer's rubber roller. We guided a bath towel or sheet carefully with both hands to distribute the bulk; otherwise it would bunch up and cause the wringer to pop open. Surely doing the washing then was much more exciting than stuffing clothes into an automatic washer now.

We hung clothes up to dry on lines made of bailing wire, strung between piñon trees. And there were rules about hanging, too: colored things were hung in the shade so they would not fade; sheets were hung on lines high enough to keep them from dragging on the ground; nothing was hung under trees that dripped pitch.

We were minimal helpers on the trips to frozen Ramah Lake to cut ice for the icebox—the kind that leaked on the floor if we forgot to empty the drip pan underneath. We helped brush snow off the ice, then just watched as 100-pound blocks were sawed, lifted with huge tongs and placed in a load of sawdust in a horse-drawn wagon. We were allowed to ride on top of the load, making "nests" to sit in so we would not bounce off the wagon as it bumped over the rough road to the ranch. The blocks of ice were buried in a huge warehouse of sawdust. When summer came, we would help dig out the blocks, which we could locate by searching for wet sawdust.

Chores were always balanced with fun. In the wintertime Mother would pack up our warm ice-skating clothes and a picnic supper and pick us up at school. We would go to the lake, sweep off the snow and skate until suppertime, then build a fire to warm the picnic supper and ourselves. Sometimes we even skated after the moon came up. Milking the cow long after sundown was definitely verboten, and we were cautioned "never to tell Daddy!" (My father was away a great deal of the time, so Mother held the reins). The plentiful pictures taken of all four of us children reminds us of how happy our parents were to have us.

Three sisters riding on a sled, pulled by our father & guided by our brother.
Ramah Lake, 1931

Moving ice blocks to the ice house - a warehouse filled with sawdust. Aunt Dor is on the left.

Vogtie, Me, Jo Ann & Patti in Navajo costumes for the Gallup Inter-Tribal Ceremonial

The present large kitchen was added in 1919, & the screened
porch was extended to meet the kitchen.

he Vogt Ranch kitchen became the heart of the house: the entrance, the greeting place, the cooking and baking and eating place, and a center for all kinds of activities—cleaning guns, oiling boots, heating water (to start a car on cold mornings), repairing tires, playing poker, churning butter, making ice cream, wrapping packages, feeding orphan lambs with a baby bottle, holding 4-H Club meetings and writing letters or doing homework.

The oven of the old Kalamazoo cookstove was, yes, for baking, but its open door was also a warm, welcome platform for drying feet or heating the carton-box "incubator" for fluffy newborn baby chicks from the Sears catalog. A washtub might be on top of the stove, full of melting snow for a child's bath in front of the living-room fireplace. Sometimes Mother rendered mutton tallow on the back of the stove so she could mix another batch of pine-tar salve, a sheepherder's cure for her eczema. In freezing weather a small clothesline stretched over the stove for drying "can't wait" items brought in from the clothesline, frozen stiff.

Along the wall of the entryway, a row of hooks at bellybutton height welcomed jackets, sweaters and sombreros of family and visitors. You know the comforting familiarity of sameness? Of finding things where they always had been? The milk bucket hanging on a bridge spike on the end of a cupboard just beyond this row of coats was one such familiar sight. I can recall almost bursting into tears one time upon returning from college to find the milk bucket in a new place.

From the window over the huge old enamel sink we could watch the comings and goings—

PINE TAR SALVE

Melquiades Tafoya. Damacio García. Antonio Arellano. Baltazar Jaramillo. Teodoro Tafoya. Epiphanio Leyba. Such beautiful names of sheepherders as listed in the Atarque Sheep Company payroll ledger. Saying these poetic names aloud made me wonder which of the men was the one with a wife who showed my mother how to make pine-tar salve for her eczema when she noticed all the bandages on her hands.

Often there would be an old wobbly baking pan on the back of the wood stove full of mutton tallow being rendered. When there was enough, the big kitchen table would be transformed into a pharmaceutical center for making this special salve. First we got out a conglomeration of empty cold-cream jars, mustard jars and jelly jars for our finished product. Next the tallow was strained into a small mixing bowl, and as it congealed, we took turns beating it with an old-fashioned eggbeater while another one of us slowly poured in heavy, smelly liquid pine tar until the mixture was just the right color, café au lait. The stuff on the beater looked fluffy and good enough to lick as we poured it into the jars. We had to do several small batches because it set pretty fast.

I am now using what I imagine is the last jar. It's in a Tussy cream-deodorant jar with a red lid, and the smell of it brings such a vivid memory of my mother. I see her standing in her nightie by the mantel of the living room fireplace, doing her bedtime bandaging with this salve.

✦

maybe Pantalio, a Navajo worker, bringing a wagon load of firewood or brother Vogtie returning on horseback from hunting for a cow on the mesa. The handmade wooden drainboards sloped slightly toward the sink, held by anchor cleats nailed to the adjacent cupboards. The cabinet underneath this sink was a putting place for the usual jumble of scrub brushes, Dutch Cleanser, and Fels Naphtha soap—oh, and the little covered wooden box for potatoes.

Above the window over the sink hung (and still hangs) a sign in fancy lettering: "Swearing Positively Forbidden Here. Not That We Give A Damn, But It Sounds Like Hell Before Strangers." Nobody remembers where our father found it.

Visualize next an old Hoosier cabinet—a bake center with a pullout counter for kneading bread, a flour bin with sifter spout, a handy space for salt, sugar, baking powder and lard. Here Mother often blitzed out a batch of biscuits for those many people my father brought home unexpectedly—interesting visitors from El Morro or perhaps just somebody whose car he had pulled out of the mud.

A propane refrigerator finally replaced the old icebox cooled by blocks of ice cut from Ramah Lake. The hot water tank in the early years was heated by a water pipe extending from the tank through the firebox of the old wood stove. This stove also had a reservoir, a covered compartment where water stayed hot for those times that the dishwashing person wished the bathers had saved a bit more.

The homemade box for fragrant cedar wood for the stove has a countertop. Now it is a space for the telephone and notepaper; long ago it held one end of the legless ironing board, while the other end went to the corner of the dining table. It was an easy step or two over to the stove to change your flatiron to a hot one as you ironed your way through the huge laundry basket of sprinkled garments.

A Navajo rug covered the trunk-style box that stored soiled clothes and linens—a comfortable bench for visitors. Navajo friends and workers simply walked in without knocking, sat down in this familiar place, and after a *Ya-ta-hey* greeting were given a cup of coffee. Often no conversation would occur until a family member inquired—knowing that was the reason for the visit—"*¿Quiere traer leña?*" (Do you want to bring firewood?) Then a deal would be made for either cedar for the cookstove or piñon for the fireplaces. A wagonload for $4 or $5 would arrive in a day or so. Later the chopping would be arranged for $1 per hour.

In the center of this kitchen is a huge homemade dining table made of 12-inch planks. It has been painted shiny black enamel for as long as I can remember, in delightful contrast to the red chair backs. A shelf underneath the table, near the floor, braces the table and serves as a footrest. I recall my childhood days before cupboards were built when this shelf held pots and pans and such. A wooden butter bowl became a toy: when I was 2 years old, I sat in the bowl with my legs out straight and Vogtie would hold my feet and whirl me around.

The kitchen's south wall has a large window overlooking the fenced garden, beyond which you can see the highway from Gallup-Zuni-Ramah to El Morro National Monument, Tinaja and Grants. Across this highway is a view of alfalfa fields, Navajo grazing land and a mesa. My sister Patti's husband, Paul Merrill, replaced a small window with the present large bay window that added to the room's cheerfulness and made space for two armchairs—ideal for cooking kibitzers, table-seating overflow or coffee sippers. Bright geraniums and hanging plants found a place in the happy, sunny area.

The west wall had a floor-to-ceiling cupboard—a gold mine of dishes, pans, Dutch oven and camp coffee pot, place mats, napkins, jelly jars with their paraffin covers and mousetraps. The gamuza hung in one corner.

The Vogt kitchen as it looks today
The photo shows me working at
one of the original cabinets.

The woodbox is to the
left of the Kalamazoo
wood-burning stove
which is still being
used along with the
Sears enamel propane
stove.

My doll Priscilla is still intact &
beautiful. Her head is made of
china; her lashed eyelids open
& close, her cheeks are pink &
chubby; she has a composition
body with dimpled arms & knees;
she wears a long-lace-edged
batiste dress with matching
bonnet, trimmed with pink satin-
ribbon bows, 1997

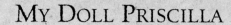
One day in 1928, when I was about 8 years old, my mother answered a knock at the door, and a visitor identified himself as the cook for workers that were connecting the first transcontinental telephone line just across the valley. He said he noticed chickens running around our yard and hoped that we would be able to provide him with 50 dressed chickens by the end of the week. Mother didn't have many fryers but managed to get more from people in the nearby town of Ramah.

I can recall the chases around the chicken pen, the wing flapping and squawking, and the dung-flavored dust flying everywhere. Strangely, even the brave job of chopping off chicken heads with the hatchet on a big tree stump—hanging the pullets from the piñon trees to drain while we boiled water for feather plucking—didn't interfere with our enjoyment then, nor even now, of fried chicken!

The distinctive smell of scalded chicken feathers rushes back to me as I visualize each chicken doused in a metal pail of hot water. The quicker we plucked after the scalding, the better, so we learned to hurry, grabbing handfuls of feathers to denude the fryers, taking out stubborn pin feathers with pliers.

I still appreciate having learned how to cut up a chicken by locating the main joints to cut between instead of cleavering at random, which it seems some of todays' butchers do. Dividing the breast into serving-size pieces was done with a huge butcher knife hit with a hammer.

The money my mother received for 50 dressed chickens was spent partly for the most exciting Christmas surprises my sister Jo Ann and I ever had: German-made baby dolls from Marshall Fields in Chicago.

EL MORRO C W A BOON TO RAMAH; BIG CREW WORKS

WASHINGTON, Jan. 3. (AP)—Destructive blizzards which killed thousands of sheep, struck at the morale of people in the vicinity of Ramah, N. M., last winter, Secretary Ickes said today, but this winter the people are facing the next few months with renewed courage as a result of a civil works program at El Morro national monument.

E. Z. Vogt, custodian of the monument, reported to Ickes that a large crew of men is now at work on a preservative development program there.

The workers include cowboys and homesteader farmers from Oklahoma and Texas who migrated to New Mexico who have been making efforts to produce crops and establish homes.

The CWA crew that worked on a project at El Morro National Monument supervised by my father in 1933.

Job Search During the Depression

When I found my father up at dawn using a hunt-and-peck system on his portable typewriter at the kitchen table, I was not aware that he was covering the United States with job applications. Our parents thought it was important to protect us as much as possible from life's harshest realities. In a letter to my mother he commented: "It's too bad Barbara saw my letter about my discouragement with job hunting."

In his files is a mass of letters inquiring about jobs. A handwritten testimonial for Palmolive Soap is witness to constant efforts to bring in a little cash: "Range men who spend long days in the open come in at night tired, dirty and sometimes hungry, tired and dirty. A good wash and bath with Palm Olive Soap cleanses, cheers and rests them more than any soap. Its invigorating powers bring zest, rest and cheer."

There is a letter from Will Rogers' agent thanking my father for his offer to send stories about interesting Indians he knew, saying he already had sufficient story materials. And more and more:
• A July 1934 letter to the Federal Emergency Relief Administration
• An August inquiry to the Agricultural Adjustment Administration to be a sheep sorter for $8 a day—deciding which sheep, suffering from the drought, were fit for food
• A draft to the Drought Relief Service of the U.S. Department of Agriculture
• A letter to the Valencia County Emergency Relief Administration about roadwork
• A reply from the president of Colliers Weekly, who was a friend, saying he knew of no immediate prospective buyers for our ranch (It was shocking

to realize that we might have had to move if my father had got the grazier job he applied for.)

• A March 1935 letter from U.S. Rep. John Dempsey referring to a letter of "loud praise" for my father from Buck Macy, head of the Highway Department and saying he regretted that he had not known of my father's availability before he had sent in his recommendations for an opening.

Rufus G. Pool of the Department of Interior received a very warm recommendation about my father from another close friend at the University of Chicago, the secretary of the board of trustees, John F. Moulds:

He is one of the most industrious, intelligent, courageous and altogether able men of my acquaintance and I admire him greatly for what he has done in the face of adverse conditions. I do not believe that you could find a finer person in the Southwest to choose for a responsible position in connection with the administration of public lands [as grazier] than Mr. Vogt. He is thoroughly honest and dependable and would make a fine public servant.

One of the interesting things about Mr. Vogt is the remarkable way in which he has kept his contact with the educational world in spite of his rather remote location. He is unusually well read and has kept fully posted on a remarkably wide range of current affairs.

One of the most promising opportunities was with the Department of Agriculture. In a letter of application for the grazier position my father says: "My very intimate experience on the range for 30 years with cattle, sheep, horses, farming, well drilling, dam building, surveying, erosion control, revegetation, raising, shipping and trading in live stock and my ability to use Spanish as well as some of the Indian languages makes me feel that I am unusually well qualified for the position." My father's devoted friend Artie Bruce spoke on his behalf to the director of grazing and was told there had been 2,000 applicants, that his status with National Park Service would not be transferable, and that he should grab anything he could get! For example, Indian land survey work.

During these probings for something permanent,

my father conducted a Civil Works Administration project at El Morro to protect the inscriptions and improve the trail over the top. Gravel for the trail, harmonious in color with the sandstone rock, was hauled by teams for eight miles, dumped at the foot of the trail and then taken by pack horses to places on the trail where needed. Grama grass transplanted in front of the historic camp cove prevented further erosion. The workers were cowboys and homesteaders who migrated from Texas and Oklahoma during the Dust Bowl days and Spanish-Americans who worked when possible in sheep and cattle outfits or lumber mills—and who had been for months without employment. They established camps in tents or dug-outs against the cliffs and bluffs and worked with pick and shovel on the check dams and erosion projects with as much energy "as though they had a chicken dinner awaiting them at their camps instead of frijoles cooked in a bean hole in hot cedar and piñon coals," reported my father to Secretary Harold L. Ickes of the Department of Interior.

Throughout it all, Mother was sweetly calm and stoic, enjoying her homemaking and mothering, keeping the ranch house Dutch clean and colorfully decorated. Even during these hard times, my father often brought unexpected guests—perhaps a stranger he had just pulled out of the mud. If it was mealtime, he would say, "Oh, just put 'em on the corner of the table and give them a fried egg if there isn't enough." So Mother would blitz out a batch of hot biscuits. The oven temperature of the old wood cook stove was determined by the size of cedar wood she put in the firebox. She tested the temperature by briefly thrusting her hand inside the oven.

The Inn (guesthouse) at the Vogt Ranch

My father's ebullient personality and enthusiasm for the beauty and wholesomeness of the Southwest was conveyed via correspondence to many friends. He invited them to come and visit and share our life, bringing rambunctious teen-agers for the summer, a mentally ill person, a convalescing friend to keep occupied and cheered up, or an alcoholic to heal, as well as many interesting, well-known and appreciative guests.

The countless people who signed the Vogt Ranch guest book reflect our home's boundless and cordial hospitality. My father so enjoyed having visitors by the fire in our colorful living room, paved with Navajo rugs, where he would share the many Indian artifacts and books on the Southwest. Among well-known visitors whose names are in the guest book are authors Oliver LaFarge, Erna Ferguson and Mary Austin; artists Gerald Cassidy and W. R. Leigh; anthropologists Bertha Dutton, John Adair, Dorothea Leighton and Arthur Woodward; National Park Service personnel Harold C. Bryant, Frank Kittredge, Jesse Nusbaum, Frank Pinkley, Horace Albright and J. B. Hamilton; New Mexico ranchers Floyd Lee and Robert Morley; historian Marc Simmons; C. T. Ripley of the Santa Fe Railroad; and Charles F. Lummis, author and director of the Southwest Museum in Pasadena.

One of the frequent guests at the Inn, our original guesthouse, was cultural anthropologist Clyde Kluckhohn, well-known researcher of and author about the Navajo Indians. Sometimes Clyde was joined by his attractive, brilliant wife Florence, who was a sociologist. They had only one child, Richard, whom I was asked to care for one summer.

CLYDE KLUCKHOHN

A DISTINGUISHED CAREER

Anthropologist Clyde Kluckhohn had become fascinated with the Navajo culture at age 17 when he came to the Vogt Ranch from his freshman year at Princeton to recuperate from an illness. The following year, 1923, he made a horseback trip to Rainbow Bridge, which resulted in his 1927 book, "To the Foot of the Rainbow." A bachelor's degree from Harvard in 1928, a Rhodes Scholarship in 1932, instructorship at University of New Mexico in 1932-34, and a doctorate from Harvard in 1936 were all stepping stones to his distinguished career. He was chairman of the Department of Anthropology at Harvard University, first president of the American Anthropology Association, one of the founders of the Laboratory of Social Relations at Harvard University and director of Harvard's Russian Research Center.

RESEARCH IN RAMAH

In 1947 his "Mirror for Man" received the McGraw Hill award for most popular work on science. His interest in value systems led to the Comparative Study of Values in Five Cultures Project, which was conducted in the Ramah Area from 1949 to 1953. Fieldworkers in various branches of behavioral science studied the Navajos, Zunis, Spanish-Americans, Mormons and Texan homesteaders.

A PROLIFIC WRITER

It is mind-boggling to realize what a prolific writer Clyde was while managing his various commitments, including being a consultant in the Office of War Information on the Japanese. His bibliography includes many reviews of articles in professional journals as well as of Oliver LaFarge's "Pictorial History of the American Indian." He was the author of numerous books on the Navajos; co-author with my brother Vogtie of a pictorial essay about the Navajos, "Navaho Means People," with photographer Leonard McCombe.

❧❧

At age 2, he was absolutely the most precocious, articulate and intelligent child I had ever known. Through Clyde, my folks met Louisa and John Wetherill, owners of the trading post in Kayenta, Ariz., who also came to visit.

Sometimes visitors presented almost insurmountable challenges. One mentally ill guest had a complete psychotic breakdown and required several people to get her into the car to be taken for treatment. In my 17th summer I was the paid companion for Latrelle, a friend's special friend, and her 10-year-old adopted daughter. Tragically, Latrelle committed suicide while the rest of us were on a picnic. She had chosen not to go along and refused my offer to stay home with her. Earlier, saying she wanted her daughter to plant some flowers by the Inn to cheer her up, she had asked for a seed catalog. With the seeds she also ordered cyanide, and her package had arrived. After several hours of chasing clues and deciphering a note left on the kitchen table, we found her under a piñon tree up the canyon. She had taken a jar of water to wet the cyanide; then had drunk it. For years I had nightmares.

I remember a typical Sunday evening when we had to scrounge up supper for 12 people. The cow milkers brought in the manurey buckets of milk to be strained and stored. Two little kiddoes were chasing a dog through the house. One of the guests was drying some of his film on a line over the stove. My father and Clyde Kluckhohn were having an animated conversation on one corner of the table where I was trying to arrange the fruit salad and a selection of sandwiches. One guest kept asking if it was time to ring the dinner bell—a brake drum from an old car. When struck with its clanger, a huge bridge spike, the bell sound could be heard for half a mile. It still hangs by bailing wire from the kitchen porch roof.

MARC SIMMONS

OFF THE GRID

A well-known historian and author of many books on the Southwest, Marc Simmons lives among the red bluffs and piñon trees off N.M. 14 south of Santa Fe in an adobe he built himself. He uses a wood stove and kerosene lamps. His only electric appliance is a television set, powered by a 15-foot cord running through a hole in the wall to his car's cigarette lighter.

WIDE-RANGING TOPICS

Marc uses a manual typewriter for his prolific writing: biographies of prominent Southwesterners, and his fascinating topics such as witchcraft, the Comanches, ironwork, outlaws, Hispanic villages and even food—piki bread of the Pueblo Indians, biscochitos and atole of the Hispanos. His articles have been published in the "New Mexico Historical Review," "Southwestern Historical Quarterly," "El Palacio," "New Mexico Quarterly," "New Mexico Magazine," "National Geographic," "Encyclopedia Americana" and the "Smithsonian's Handbook of North American Indians."

MANY HONORS

Born in Dallas, Texas, Marc first visited New Mexico at age 12, returning for many subsequent childhood summers. He graduated from the University of Texas with a major in Latin American Studies, received a master's in Inter-American Affairs at the University of New Mexico in 1960 and a doctorate in history in 1965. He has translated old volumes of Spanish documents and assisted in cataloging the Spanish archives of New Mexico. For his documentation of Spanish history in New Mexico, Spain awarded him the Order of Isabela la Católica. Because of his intriguing stories about the Santa Fe Trail, he is a popular speaker at historical societies and other gatherings.

A FASCINATING LIFE

He has been a ranch hand in Wyoming, a farrier, a horse wrangler, a movie extra with Warner Brothers, a Peace Corp trainer and an assistant professor at the University of New Mexico and Colorado College. In recent years Marc has spent considerable effort fighting off developers from his pristine area.

Above L to R: Jane Wetherill, co-author of "Traders to the Navajos," & John Wetherill with Mother & Father at the Wetherill home & trading post in Kayenta, Arizona, 1930

At left: Father & Dr. Frederick Hodge, director of the Museum of the Southwest in Los Angeles, here sitting on top of El Morro, 1930

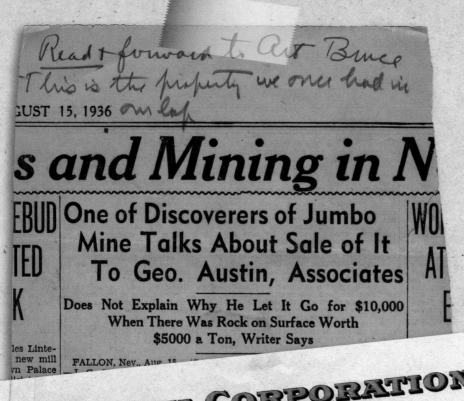

Read & forward to Art Bruce

This is the property we once had in on lap

AUGUST 15, 1936

s and Mining in N

WANTED

EBUD

TED

K

les Linte-
new mill
vn Palace

One of Discoverers of Jumbo
Mine Talks About Sale of It
To Geo. Austin, Associates

Does Not Explain Why He Let It Go for $10,000
When There Was Rock on Surface Worth
$5000 a Ton, Writer Says

FALLON, Nev., Aug. 15

WO

AT

E

proximately
a day, with a ton and a half mill.
"It's in the Awakening district in
the Slumbering hills," Stagg said,
out, a property that showed seams

not apply.
He is still running ore through the
one and one-half ton mill.. Tailings
from the mill are shipping ore. They
run $30 to $40 a ton.
Some of the rich streaks are showing

federal
district
take it
ing er

Wit
minir
peate
acte

A.O. SMITH CORPORATION
MANUFACTURERS OF STEEL PRODUCTS
MILWAUKEE, WISCONSIN

GOLD-MINING EXPLORATION

In 1935 while doing some work at Chaco Canyon and Wupatki national monuments, my father was contacted by longtime friend Ray Smith of the A.O. Smith Corporation who offered him a job scouting for gold mines in the Southwest and in Mexico, using Ray's exciting new gold-refining method. My father accepted the job and during explorations in Nevada, Colorado, Arizona, Utah and Mexico, he wrote a 118-page journal as well as numerous letters to the family describing adventures, hardships and hopes. They include vivid descriptions of views and vegetation and geology as well as of people he worked with and encountered in his travels.

His first project was buying a car. Next was getting outfitted with a chuck box (wooden box to hold camping supplies), cooking equipment including Dutch oven, an old-fashioned bedroll in a new tarp, sheep pelts (to use as a mattress), a tow chain, a shovel and ax, and things for personal survival as well as for coping with uncertain roads and changing weather conditions.

He talked to deans of mining schools for leads and information, to mining engineers for technical information. In each mining town he contacted old-timers and prospectors as well as prestigious, influential persons who could help him evaluate the politics and economics of the area and the character of the present owner of each mine. He once went to the head of the Spanish department at the University of Arizona for a letter of reference to a prominent lawyer in Mexico he hoped would help him with negotiations. He was greatly concerned about safety of any investment in Mexico since some thought the country was on the brink of revolution. With each mine visited, he had to consider climate, shipping conditions and labor supply.

Almost daily, letters came to my mother or to one of us children with such advice as, "Be sweet to each other. Do what your mother wants." Postcards arrived sharing the latest of his whereabouts. He tracked down and visited old friends in the path of his travels.

He frequently went to Lake Tahoe to meet with Ray Smith at the Henry Kaiser Lodge. Henry, one of the builders of Hoover Dam, was a close associate of Ray's. Many times my father went for consultation to Ray's home in Pasadena where he luxuriated at an elegant hotel, ate at the Huntington Hotel and longed to share it all with my mother.

A staff member once told my father that he was being trained for one of the big jobs with Smith Exploration Corporation. My father's letter reported the conversation. "He said I was one of the best mixers and contact men he had ever met and that the beauty of it was that I could sit down on the ground and roll a cigarette and talk with a campesino in Mexico just as well as make myself easy with a Wall Street banker." My father's reaction: "I was so

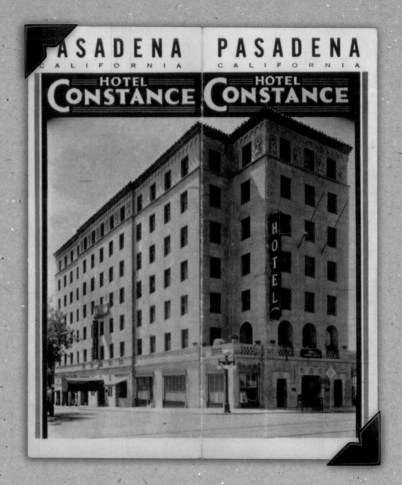

Brochure from the Constance Hotel. My Father stayed there while consulting with Ray Smith in Pasadena.

delighted I shed tears when he told me. I am so deter-mined to make a killing in this great undertaking that I can hardly sleep … made three times as many contacts of value than I would have needed to and think I have turned up some properties which will lead the Company into millions!"

Many complications are reported in the daily jour-nal and in the family letters: flat tires and mechanical problems with the car, including a boiling radiator in 140-degree heat. His bedroll disappeared, his wallet was stolen by a hotel maid. Once in Nevada he had no money for food because of refusals to cash his A.O. Smith expense check. He finally spotted political and economic titan George Wingfield, recognizing him from newspaper photos. Wingfield, who made a for-tune in gold mining in Nevada, OK'd the check—he owned the hotel where my father was staying.

Once late at night my father got stuck in the sand while driving to the train depot in order to meet an incoming Smith Corporation engineer early the next morning. Being too tired to dig out the car, he put his sheep pelts down and, after a good night's rest, got some helpers and dug the car out early the next morning.

Tidbits gleaned from his correspondence, mostly letters to family, include the following.

• "Thanks for sending pajama top, but when I sleep I only wear a smile."

• He spent six months at Summitville mine in Colorado where he got experience in mining, ware-housing, milling, timbering, shipping gold bullion. Here, after attending a dance, he discovered some of the crew got drunk and ate the 27 box lunches the head cook had made for the miners for the following day. "I may have to put on a cook's apron and go to work!"

• He hiked in 120-degree heat up to a mine to exam-ine it. Exhausted.

• Near Virginia City, he got the help of an Italian farmer to dig three holes 4 feet deep to bury a 16-pound bell in one of the holes for an engineer from Milwaukee headquarters to prove his machine could detect metal! The engineer never arrived, and he had to dig up the dumb bell.

• He made constant apologies for not getting home to visit and to help and expressed anxiety regarding news from home about Buck McDaniel shooting the

Colorado sheriff and fleeing to New Mexico, where it was feared he was hiding out near the ranch in ice-cave country.

• "All I can do is stay here and use my noggin to land this rich mine for Ray. I'm certain that it will produce literally millions."

• Eventually, the A.O. Smith engineers turned down the "greatest strike in modern times"—a giant disappointment. (I recall a letter telling us that the assayist in San Francisco rejected the most promising discovery as "not being rich enough," but according to a follow-up letter, a South African gold-mining outfit purchased the property for millions!)

• June 1936: A.O. Smith now employs about 500 men at Round Mountain, Nev., working on sampling and starting construction on a 250-ton pilot mill.

• July 1937: "A.O. Smith mining operations have shut down. I am watchman (at a decreased salary) of equipment until it is sold off. I am the only one here with the hoot owls and pack rats." This comment reflects his irrepressible sense of humor in spite of the disappointments and problems.

• He even considered leasing the Vogt Ranch and moving the family to Round Mountain to keep him company while the Smith Exploration Company was on the countdown.

While home from the Nevada job, he wrote on April 12, 1937, to Bill Wrather, one of the investors in Atarque Sheep Company, reassuring Bill that he was keeping up the ranch, which he had given as his share of investment in the Atarque company:

I have spent nearly every day here on work around the Ranch so that it will be kept up in good shape. The severe wind blew off a lot of the new roofing paper on the guest cabin. This I put on again with hot tar and plenty of roofing nails. Connected the water with the cabin. Repaired the sewer to the arroyo after digging up the line at half a dozen places. Put Delco plant and pump in good shape. Worked over two miles of wire boundary fence as well as the canyon field fence. Also cut brush along Coal Canyon and up on the mesa two days with a Navajo to repair the drift fences there. I have the place pretty cattle-tight now so that the grass can be protected.

Father's adventure in gold-mining ended in 1938.

other courageously coped with all the complications, as revealed by these gleanings from her letters to my father when he was working in Colorado and Nevada for the Smith Exploration Company:

• "The water pump is broken. Vogtie, Lavelle and Paul got it running but it won't pump water. Finally Billy Ducket [nearby rancher] got a new valve and fixed it while others drew water by bucket for horses and brought in wood for me."

• "The drain is stopped up and ground too frozen to dig for trouble spot, so we're slinging used water out the door. The kids complain about no bath until Spring, but that's not as bad as a broken water pump or sick Delco motor."

• "Relying on Billy Ducket and Larry Emert [school-teacher] to fix things for me."

• "Faithful Yazzie is bringing wood and Procopio is chopping it."

• "I sent your shirts after sewing the raggedy edges of the sleeves and turning the collars."

• "I wish I had ordered baby chicks and planted a garden, but you were so sure we would move to Colorado when school was out." [I even boarded with a family in Monte Vista and attended school there for a while and Mother went up and looked at a home to rent.]

• "The puppy got into porcupine quills."

• "The roof is leaking. Mr. Dent paid for roofing."

• "We are out of wood-burning chips and Yazzie is not at his hogan."

• "No horse. No car. Too hot to walk to the post office."

• "It will probably rain today since the alfalfa is cut!"

• "Some drunkards let the cow out of the pasture."

• "Eczema on my hands is bad. I'm allergic to the stuff the doctor gave Barby for her boils!"

DEAR DADDY
MAMMA IS SICK IN BED
AND HAD THE DR.
I WENT TO GRANDMA'S
TO TELL THEM TO CALL
THE DR. I WENT TO GET
A WOMAN TO HELP US. BUT
SHE CAN'T COME TILL THIS
AFTER NOON. GRANDMA'S
COMING TO GET OUR LUNCH
WISH YOU WERE HERE
WITH US   WITH LOVE
VOGTIE

Father traveled frequently on
business. This letter to him from
Vogtie dated May 15, 1925, shows
how much we missed him while he
was away.

• "I rode pregnant Prieta today looking in vain for Roanie who finally came in at the end of the day for a drink."

• "Busy getting Vogtie settled at El Morro for his job as ranger. Cleaned rugs and curtains in the ranger cabin and got new oil cloth for the table."

• "We have been asked to care for little Dickie Kluckhohn (son of Clyde and Florence Kluckhohn). Not sure parents would approve putting him to sleep in the car during ball game and dance at Zuni."

• "Colt was lost. We found him way out by Dog Lake."

• "Patti let Roanie out with saddle still on. It was a merry chase, but finally got the help of a Navajo at the well."

• "Drain stopped up again. Emert is digging."

• "Barbara concerned about where she will be going to school. She says, "Dickie is positively the most quick-minded, most inquisitive child I ever expect to see or hear. Judging from his knowledge at two years, I think he'll be a genius at 20. I spend hours every day with him and enjoy him as much as any grown-up."

• "The little mule who takes your hat off and drops it on the ground several feet away also nibbles at the seat of your pants."

• "The cow won't come in to be milked. Can't keep Roanie in corral all the time, have to go after her. Snorty is at El Morro with Vogtie."

• "The telephone line is down, the chicken house is alive with mites, and the sewer is stopped up again. I don't know which way to turn. I will be glad when you get home to help us. We always hope every day some definite news will come from you."

My mother accepted the horrendous condition of my father's clothes when he returned during the mining adventure: "I know that was my new shirt but I had to use it to wrap some valuable ore specimens." And then, attempting to console Mother with humor: "I washed it and borrowed an iron but I couldn't figure out how to get the iron inside the sleeves!"

Poker games were a happy diversion when my father was away. My grandmother Kate was probably the impetus. She visited often from Santa Fe where she played poker with the prominent Greer family in their charming home on the corner of Don Gaspar and Paseo de Peralta. One of our special family friends was

Homer Powers of Gallup, the McKinley County agricultural extension agent, a veterinarian, who came to the ranch often to advise us about ranching matters, especially sick cows and horses. He often stayed over for an evening game of poker. I remember falling asleep to the sounds of laughter and screaming when five aces beat out a bluff!

This merriment was without any liquor, which was never in our home in those days because my father strongly opposed it. It was once said, "He didn't even welcome anybody who had ever smelled a cork!" Refreshments were served at the end of the game, around midnight. In the years of the Depression, my mother would prepare a tray of white soda crackers with grated cheese on top, melted in the oven!

Other friends who were usually part of the poker parties were Grace and Ray Shepherd, who ran the Ramah Trading Company and whose children were our playmates. I remember vividly, too, the musical evenings when Grace played 1920s tunes on our piano, Shep (Ray) played his saxophone, and Mother the banjo. They decided once that they had perfected enough selections to hold a dance on a summer evening in the ranch house. They invited friends from "up the canyon" and from Ramah.

When we were teens, Homer Powers asked Mother to be a 4-H Club leader. The four H's stand for Head (knowledge), Heart (caring), Hands (skills) and Health. While Mother was the home-economics leader for this group, she improved her knowledge of sewing, which had previously been limited to mending and darning. In addition she developed sewing ingenuity while remodeling clothes given to us by Agnes Smith, who could afford to buy very stylish and well-made clothes for her daughters and pass them along to us. In her later years Mother enjoyed making from patterns many beautiful outfits for herself as well as wedding dresses for granddaughters, always on her faithful old Singer treadle machine, which is still being used at the Vogt Ranch.

The highlight of this 4-H experience was when Mother's demonstration team, Laverne Davis and myself, won the state championship at the state agricultural college at Las Cruces. Requirements for the contest were that both members must be working during the 20 minutes allotted—that is, peeling, pouring, measuring and stirring while spoken instructions were alternated between the two partners, so it required lots of concentration and practice. Making several salads and also mayonnaise, we tied with a team of boys preparing breakfast, so the demonstrations had to be repeated for the judges. Homer was along and helped solve the problem of how to get our jello salad molded in the brief time until the final judging: use ice instead of water to dilute the jello after it is dissolved. We were chosen by the judges over the breakfast makers in spite of the fact that, remembering Mother's warning that dashes of paprika used to garnish the dollop of mayonnaise topping a salad must never be sprinkled onto the plate, I picked up the plate on which I had goofed, and, within 2 feet of the judges, blew off the paprika!

Our Navajo neighbor, Bertha Alonzo, helped us with the laundry, 1930.

THE GALLUP GAZETTE

Published Every Thursday

VOLUME 8 — NUMBER 43

GALLUP, N. M., THURSDAY, AUGUST, 20, 1942

GALLUP
THE INDIAN CAPITAL

5 CENTS

Ed Houghton Out For | New Mexico Cowboys Are Joining New | Baptists Purchase

Father in the office of the "Gallup Gazette." He found the skull in an alley in Gallup, 1940.

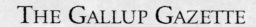

At the conclusion of the gold-mining venture, my father returned to New Mexico and bought the weekly *Gallup Gazette,* which he edited from 1938 to 1942. He kept an apartment in Gallup, coming to the ranch when he could. During these "newspaper times," he was president of the Gallup Rotary Club, president of the Gallup Chamber of Commerce and secretary of the Gallup Inter-Tribal Indian Ceremonial while honorary vice presidents were Charles F. Lummis, Neil Judd of the National Museum of Washington, Edgar Hewitt of Santa Fe, A.V. Kidder of the Peabody Museum at Harvard, and Jesse Nusbaum, then superintendent of Mesa Verde National Park.

Involved as he was with newspaper and civic duties, he always found time to help someone in need. Once at his newspaper office, a policeman delivered to him a note from a Navajo friend in jail, penciled on a torn piece of brown paper bag. As requested, he got the man out of jail by promising the judge that he himself would serve the rest of the man's jail time if he failed to return in 10 hours. The man returned in only seven hours, having taken care of his horse that he had left tied to a tree half way to Ramah. He also had gotten some jewelry from his hogan to pawn in order to pay off a fine.

Following are gleanings from the *Gallup Gazette* while my father was the editor that give a taste of the times.

• Though there were fewer California visitors, the mines were working, the trains were running, buildings were going up, and supplies were going out to the trading posts.

• Navajo-gathered piñon nuts increased in popularity.

- Wartime travelers' need for cafes, hotels and car services helped the local economy.
- A 1941 editorial pointed out that visiting soldiers needed welcome, food and information about the unique region. Another editorial encouraged the clearance of slums and replacement with new low-cost housing.
- The PEO women's service club was making charity boxes for the needy.
- M'Lockers, the dry goods store, advertised "house slippers for 89 cents and up."
- Mason's Stationery Store had copper Christmas cards for 5 cents and 10 cents.
- Rent for small homes was $12 to $50 a month.
- In November 1941, Mary Wheelwright visited with Roman Hubbell, prominent Indian trader, and interviewed Navajo medicine men for ceremonial chant material.
- Because of the spectacular red rock mesas and the availability of all kinds of "characters" for extras, many films were made in Gallup: 1940—*The Bad Man* with Wallace Beery and Ronald Reagan; 1941— *Sundown* with Gene Tierney and Bruce Cabot and *The Desert Song* with Dennis Morgan. These were shown at the El Morro Theatre.
- The Fort Wingate Ordinance Depot for storage of ammunition was dedicated, with Gov. John Miles in attendance.
- The Gallup Municipal Band went to the San Francisco World's Fair.
- A Greyhound Bus Depot was established.
- Some Navajo visitors to Gallup saw their first train and their first Negro.
- The Gallup Museum was being organized and W.R. Leigh donated a painting.
- The Red Cross appealed for more knitters.
- A frigate named the *U.S.S. Gallup* was commissioned.
- 200 Navajo marines became Code Talkers.
- Gallup refused Japanese Internment Orders, saying their residents of Japanese descent were all fine citizens. Hershey Mijamura who served in the war was awarded a Medal of Honor.
- Because of gasoline rationing, people trudged to jobs, schools, movie theaters, grocery stores and errands.
- A subscription to the weekly *Gallup Gazette* was $2 a year.

Mr. E. Z. Vogt.
Will you please
help me out and
see if you could
let me out of jail
here at the city jail.
I had tied my
horse on the
high way. Yesterday
afternoon I just
worrying about the
horse. I like to
get there tonight
if I can.
Resp,
David

Please return this I want it to, put in the book
I write when I get 10 years older
    I got him out of jail at 6 am so he could go
take his horse that hadnt eaten for 30 hours, tied
in hidden grove near turnoff to Two Wells . I promi
mised judge to serve out the 7 days remaining
in jail if David did not come back within 10
hours He got here in 7 and paid his way to liberty
by pawning his jewelry to Judge and with $ 3 he
had hidden at his hogan.

Notes Father saved for his scrapbook

89

A picture of me milking Bossie when I was 16, 1936

"Crying as though the cow had died" is an expression my father used. I understood the true meaning of it one day while a student at Stanford University when news from home told me that our milk cow, Bossie, had died. I cried so hard that my roommates thought that surely I had lost my mother or my father. They didn't understand why she was such a beloved member of the family. She was gentle and faithful—almost always coming back to the corral at milking time—and produced delicious, rich milk with lots of cream, so patient as we squeezed and squirted and jerked away while learning how to milk.

The following letter, which my mother wrote on May 25, 1938, to my father in Nevada, does indeed convey as much concern and importance as though she were writing about a human being.

Dearest Daddy:

We are all so grief-stricken here, I can hardly write. Bossie died! And we worked so hard over her. I am getting so discouraged here by myself trying to do things to the best of my ability, and everything goes haywire. I suppose it might have happened even if you or Vogtie had been here. But I am always so helpless and have to run after somebody in Ramah. I don't know whether she got some weed or whether it was the corn chops she foundered on, but she got into the stable during the night Saturday night or early Sunday morning and tipped over the bran barrel. We couldn't tell how much she had eaten but she seemed all right Sunday, and Monday we didn't see her, but Homer [veterinarian-agricultural extension agent] said he came by the corral about five o'clock p.m., and she was standing there, and he looked at her especially as he went by, but didn't see anything wrong with her. She evidently wandered away again before Jo Ann went down to feed her and Tuesday morning I drove up the canyon to hunt her and found her over across the arroyo from cliff dwellings under that big pine and looking bloated up to me, though I've never seen a badly bloated cow and hardly knew what it would look like. So I went after Mr. Merrill and he and Hank Clawson came out and looked at her, didn't seem to think she was alarmingly sick, but we gave her a pound of salts. She was standing up but wouldn't move and we couldn't get her down to the corral, so just had to doctor her up there, carrying buckets of water way across the arroyo to her and everything. Then, as we had planned, we took Jo Ann into town [Gallup] to go to the Prom, so we decided to go talk to Homer about her. Mr. Merrill promised to look after her in our absence. This morning we came back and gave her another pound of salts under Homer's advice, and she had been down, but got up and walked around some, and at 4:00 this afternoon we thought her much better as the salts was acting and she was vomiting and I thought she'll surely get rid of whatever she had. Then we tried again to get her to travel poco a poco to the corral or at least get her on this side of arroyo. She'd take a few steps and that was all, so we left her, thinking she was getting better and might come on down, but her legs were quivering and she looked pretty terrible. Then we went back up about 5:30 this evening and as we drove within sight of her I said 'Oh, look, Jo Ann, she is trying to come home.' I saw a black object on this side of arroyo, but when I drew a little closer my heart stopped, for I saw she was down and, by her position, knew she had died. The poor thing was trying to come home to the corral!

"It is no joke that you used to say, 'You are crying like the cow had died,' for we certainly did all cry . . . and still feel like it. I have tried to feel she is JUST A COW, but to think we shall never hear Bossie's bell coming clanging again! It's awful and what shall we do for milk? Of course, Bossie was getting old and I knew it would happen some time, but not like that. I surely hate to write Barbara the news. It is bad enough for anyone to lose a valuable milk cow because of its value, but no one loved their cows like we did Bossie!

Later Mother wrote: "We are still mourning, and will forever, the loss of our dear Bossie. Every time I mention her Jo Ann says, 'Mother! Don't talk about her. I can't stand it!' We still can't realize the truth."

After the newspaper-publishing period, my father decided to apply for a permanent position as custodian of El Morro National Monument. An article published in a National Park Service bulletin in January 1936 explains my father's love and appreciation of El Morro and intensifies our understanding of how deep his disappointment must have been that he could not become the permanent custodian because he was too old to enter the Civil Service required for permanent federal employees.

The National Park Service decision makers would not waive this regulation despite letters from prominent people describing my father's extraordinary qualifications for the job as well as his many years of dedication to preserving and publicizing the monument: his fight for improved roads to increase access to El Morro; his research into types of preservative covering for the carved inscriptions; and efforts to publicize the monument—he even sent El Morro pamphlets to TransWorld Airlines so that stewards could point out El Morro to passengers as they flew over and hand out pamphlets to inspire visits to El Morro.

He wrote articles about El Morro and the nearby ice caves, which he also fought to preserve.

Following is a list of some of his articles:

• "El Morro National Monument," *El Palacio*, 1922, Vol. XII, PP. 161-68

• "The Ice Caves and Vagaries of Volcanoes," *El Palacio*, 1924, Vol. XVI, PP. 35-39

• "Inscription Rock," by Charles Fletcher Lummis and Evon Z. Vogt, *El Palacio*, 1926, Vol. XXI, PP. 232-37

• "El Morro National Monument," *El Palacio*,

Below, a photo of El Morro National Monument, taken by Mark Nohl for "New Mexico Magazine."

Above, one of the inscriptions carved onto the rock face. The Spanish & its translation below:

Aqui estuvo el General Don Diego
de Vargas, quien conquistó
a nuestra Santa Fe y a la Real
Corona todo el Nuevo
México a su costa, Año de 1692

Here was the General Don Diego
de Vargas, who conquered
for our Holy Faith, and for the Royal
Crown, all of New
Mexico at his own expense, Year of 1692

Translation courtesy of National Park Service's Western Archaeological Center

1927, Vol. XXIII, P. 46

• "Autographs in Stone," *New Mexico Magazine*, May 1935, reprinted in *This Is New Mexico* by George Fitzpatrick.

• "El Morro—A Camping Ground on the First Highway in the Southwest," *Arizona Highways*, 1924.

One special friend who wrote to Harold Ickes, secretary of the interior, was Dr. Frederick W. Hodge, well-known archaeologist who was excavating at Hawiku, near Zuni. Hodge's letter said: "Before an allowance for the expense of protecting this monument from vandalism was made, I know that Mr. Vogt contributed of his time and private means beyond what he could really afford, solely through his patriotic desire to preserve the early Spanish inscriptions that form an historic record of vast importance." And, "It is a pity that after years of service in behalf of El Morro and the National administration, Mr. Vogt should be replaced by reason of a regulation which must result in a detriment rather than a benefit to the National Park Service."

My father felt the same about El Morro as Lawrence Clark Powell, who says in the introduction to his *Southwest Classics* that El Morro is the "heart of hearts" (having described Arizona and New Mexico as the heartland of the Southwest). Powell wrote:

> *West southwest a half day's journey (from Albuquerque) stands El Morro, the buff-colored sandstone battlement called by the Anglos Inscription Rock and preserved since 1906 as a National Monument by act of President Theodore Roosevelt against all enemies save two—the wind and the rain. 'Here I shall haunt,' prophesied writer Mary Austin, and I just might join her. When the rest of the Southwest has fallen to Progress, I pray that El Morro will stand inviolate as a sanctuary for those who seek peace and quiet on a clean earth.*

We always enjoyed my father's interesting accounts published in a National Park Service bulletin. Here is a sample written during the unprecedented snowstorm of 1931:

> *Custodian Vogt of the El Morro National Monument gave the following vivid account of the terrible storms which caused so much suffering to Indians in the locality*

and wrought such havoc among the cattle and sheep herds: "This country is still in the bitter grasp of an awful winter. Deep snow, deeper drifts, weak sunshine and the nights as cold as thirty below. Travel has been entirely held up on main highways several times, while our road from Ramah to Gallup is penetrated by mail trucks but several times a week instead of daily.

"In the immediate neighborhood of El Morro the sheep herds belonging to Silvester Mirabal were caught in deep snow. They were trailed out finally to San Rafael and warmer country but are reported to have suffered terribly and have died by the hundreds. Our own situation at Atarque is still bad, six of our herds are able to graze fairly well but three are in deep snow country and are showing some loss. I have a supply of cottonseed cake on hand but cannot get in any more owing to the deep snow.

"The thousand or so Navajos who were picking pinon nuts on our range finally all got out but left under terrible privation despite relief in the way of food and horse feed sent to them by Indian superintendents.

"After the first snow I was unable to reach Atarque except by Government relief wagons of which I was put in charge. It took two days to reach Atarque from Zuni through the deep snow. En route we passed over 600 Navajos, some camped, some traveling afoot, horseback, or in wagons. We gave food and feed to all the most desperate ones, but they were losing lots of horses from cold and starvation. I was glad to snuggle up close to a Zuni Indian driver in his bed that night as I did not have my bed roll with me.

"We are hoping for a few warm days to melt the snow so our outfit of sheep can live."

I recall vividly one of the most picturesque visitors to El Morro, a gentleman in rumpled corduroy suit, wearing a red bandana on his head and using another bandana to make a hobo-style bundle of his minimum essentials, which he tied to a branch he carried over his shoulder as he walked across the country. This was Charles F. Lummis, photographer, editor, explorer, founder of the Southwest Museum in Pasadena, whom my father met at El Morro. Lummis visited the Ranch and El Morro on many occasions and appreciated my father's knowledge and enthusiasm about this "Stone Autograph Album," as reflected in the notation on the flyleaf of his book *Mesa, Canyon and Pueblo*, a birthday gift to my father.

When my father failed to become permanent director at El Morro, he began his final job for the Indian Service as supervisor of the Ramah Navajos, paid for many of the things he used to do for them as a friend, such as explaining ration books, advising about draft notices, etc. He fixed up a little office in the former garage by adding a floor, wood stove and windows. His typing table was a rickety affair—a table on which steaks were sawed from a hindquarter of beef when it was on our back porch!

Charles F. Lummis, author, editor, historian, poet & librarian

C. E. LORD, SANTA FE, 1926

GOD LOVE US EVERY ONE— AND PITY THEM THAT DON'T

To Evon & Shirley Vogt, with gentle memories Always Your Friend Chas. F. Lummis—

97

Picnic party on top of El Morro in 1918. Mother in hat with baby Vogtie, her sister Dorothy on her right, my father on her left. Four visitors from the Museum of the American Indian in NYC: F.W. Hodge, standing & Ed Coffin, Mr. Pepper, & one unidentified person.

Opposite, pages from "Autographs in Stone," an article my father wrote about El Morro that was published in "New Mexico Magazine,," May 1935.

Autographs in Stone

(Continued from Page 11)

Morro, for emigrants, ranchmen, soldiers, ... on the sides of the cliff. There were ... later travelers. ... Dodge, father of Chee Dodge ... jo Council chairman, dated ... od, '67-'68; General R. L. ... A. Carr, Lieut. McCook, ... at Zuni, '62; Major J. R. ... uy, Santa Fe 1873; Mar- ... , P. Gilmor, Breckinridge, ... train; Isaac T. Holland, ...

Autographs . . . in Stone

By Evon Z. Vogt
(Custodian, El Morro National Monument)

LIGHTING a big black cigar, Charles F. Lummis settled comfortably under the reading lamp in our ranch living room and in his painstaking script began writing a tribute to the two places he loved so well—El Morro and Acoma.

It was past midnight. We had spent the evening listening to Lummis' tales of frontier days in the eighties. Finally the children got sleepy, then the rest of us. But for Charley Lummis the day had just begun.

Throughout the night, with his ever present black cigar, he labored at his writings.

He filled an entire page in the visitors' register from El Morro National Monument I had brought in for him from the Rock. Then he worked on other writings until dawn.

When I awakened he had gone to bed. The big register lay open on the table.

This is what he had written:

Nowhere else does geology open to the layman so obvious, so dramatic, and so spectacular a page as in that region which I christened, 40 years ago, by the name it bears today—The Southwest. There is no other cross-section of earth building sequences as in the Grand Canyon; nor is there elsewhere on the earth such an exposition of earth-carving forces as the unique *Mesa* country of northwestern New Mexico, with its vast waves of red or fawn or grey Navajo sand-stone, breaking off in sheer and lofty cliffs; its lofty table-topped islands-in-the-air which are left in valleys to witness the far day when no valleys were, but one vast upland of triassic sand-stone; its "Monumental" erosion, prophesied by its jointing in an ancient uplift, sketched by frosts and ardent suns, turned, carved, chiselled, sand-papered by flood, rain, and wind. The world has many freaks, wonders of erosion; but it has nothing else to compare with this great area of water and wind erosion of the Navajo sandstone.

I believe there is no question that the two most interesting rocks in the world—counting their picturesque, intricate, and fantastic erosion and their historic associations—are in this formation, Acoma, The Sky City, a pueblo still living as Coronado found it in 1540, east of the Zuni Mountains or Continental Divide (whose up-humping broke the great sandstone blanket) ; and on the west, El Morro, *La Mesa Escrita*, Inscription Rock, "The Stone Autograph Album." So far as I can learn, no other cliff on earth records so much—or a tithe as much—of Romance, Adventure, Hero-

ism. Certainly all other rocks in America, do not, all together, hold so much of American history. Oñate here carved his entry with dagger two years before an English-speaking person had built a hut anywhere in the New World, 15 years before Plymouth Rock.

No other description so brief has ever said as much, and Lummis meant every word of it. He loved the country so well he seemed a part of it.

To Lummis must be given credit for bringing the grandeur of the Southwest to the attention of the American public. His "Strange Corners of Our Country," "Land of Poco Tiempo," "Mesa, Canyon and Pueblo" and other books opened for readers new vistas.—A country that seemed to many a barren, desert land became clothed with new charm.

Lummis visited El Morro first in 1885, and the last time in 1926, with numerous visits in between.

Although Lummis popularized El Morro, the "stone autograph album" was really discovered for the outside world by Lieut. J. H. Simpson and R. H. Kern, who, with their orderly, W. Bird, and a Navajo trader named Lewis, visited El Morro on September 17 and 18, 1849 and copied the inscriptions.

Their report describing the inscriptions, the petroglyphs left by early Indians, and the great ruined pueblos on top of the cliff, was published in book form in 1850 in "Reports to the Secretary of War, Including an Expedition Into the Navajo Country." Lithographs, some of them in color, made from Kern's sketches, illustrate the volume.

In ages past the Indians used the sand stone face of the castle-like rock to tell their story in petroglyphs. The *conquistadores*, seeking the *Seven Golden Cities of Cibola*, and blazing trails into new country, found the great rock sentinel on their path. Here they stopped to camp in a sheltered cove and left a record of their passing for others who followed.

Coronado passed here in 1540. No carved record of his expedition has been found, but like others inscribed during the next century it may have been obliterated.

The date and names of the Chamiscado party of the Rodriguez expedition of 1581 were noted by Bandelier and Cushing in the eighties, but they have since been effaced or obliterated.

The oldest inscription that still may be read is that

rs to the avenging of the murder of the Padre Le Trado, Lujan."

ring there is still a large pine tree that grows high against the cliff. In those early days there were many more. The marks in the cliff 50 feet above ground where swaying limbs cut into the stone prove there was much more shade then than now.

The first inscription you see after you leave your car, fifty yards away under the giant pine is that of Lujan, who headed the expedition sent to Hawikuh to punish the Zunis for killing their priest:

"He passed on the 23 of March of 1632 years to the avenging of the murder of the Priest Le Trado, Lujan."

Hawikuh, 12 miles from Zuni, chief city of Cibola when Coronado came in 1540, is in ruins today. This mission was founded by Governor Francisco Manuel de Silva Nieto, who, with his ten wagon expedition, made the trip from Santa Fe to Zuni in the summer of 1629. The carved record of the journey is in iambic verse, with letters two inches high:

"Here passed the Governor Don Francisco Manuel de Silva Nieto who has the impossible overcome with his indubitable arm and his valor with the wagons of the King, our Lord, A thing which he alone was able to bring about. On the 9 of August, 1629. That it might be well to Zuni I passed and established the Faith."

At least twenty-seven parties of Spaniards camped at El Morro between 1605 and 1774. The phrase *paso por aqui* became a customary notation.

There are no dated carvings for the period between 1774 and 1849, but after Lieut. Simpson took news of his discovery to Santa Fe there seems to have been a recurrence of travel via El

(Continued on Page 37)

---

visited and copied these inscriptions, September 17th/18th 1849.

R. H. Kern, Aug. 29 1851

---

of Don Juan de Oñate, the first governor and colonizer of New Mexico.

Over an old pictograph on the smooth face of the cliff, Oñate carved his record:

"Here passed the Adelantado Don Juan de Oñate from the discovery of the Sea of the South on the 16 of April of 1605."

Seven years before, Oñate and his little band of colonizers had struggled across desert and mountain trails and had set up the first cross in the Indian Pueblo of San Juan. There they built homes, and, across the Rio Grande, started the first white settlement and capital of the new territory, San Gabriel. Five years later they founded Santa Fe and made it the capital.

In 1620 when the Pilgrims were establishing their civilization on the eastern coast New Mexico's fifth governor was recording his activities in stone:

"The captain general of the provinces of New Mexico ...

"The Captain General of the Provinces of New Mexico for the 29th day of July, 1620, and he put them in peace at their req... all of which he did with sagacity, zeal and prudence as a mos...

My wedding in the Vogt Ranch living room on Christmas day, 1940.
L to R: Jo Ann, me & Larry, Bill Berreyesa.

My Wedding

My wedding was not the first at the Vogt Ranch. A local cowboy had been matched and married there to a childhood chum of my mother's. When prim and proper "old maid" Dottie came visiting from Chicago, my father would ask Jack Wilson, a capable, polite but very shy neighbor, to bring a gentle horse and teach Dottie how to ride. After several summers and many riding lessons, my folks succeeded in convincing the two that a lifetime of companionship would be happy and comforting, so a simple wedding ceremony took place at the ranch. Dottie's oversize antique heirloom furniture was installed in Jack's tiny, dirt-floored cabin at the foot of the Zuni Mountains.

My marriage to Larry Bell, a Stanford engineering student, was on Christmas Day 1940, midway between quarters of our junior year. We had met while waiting tables at my dormitory, and our first date was to an ice-skating rink in San Francisco. I had moved to Palo Alto to finish high school since courses at Ramah High School, which was not accredited, would not qualify for college admission. I lived with a family, helping out in exchange for room and board. Encouraged by an English teacher to apply for admission to Stanford, I was accepted and made it through with scholarships, student-aide work, a $25 monthly gift from friends of my father, and that job waiting tables in a dorm that led me to Larry.

He enchanted me with poems recited while we canoed, with the story of his parents' falling in love at Stanford in 1916, and by his asking me to marry him while we were on a hike, presenting me with an "engagement ring" crafted from a pine needle!

Our Christmas Day wedding was loaded with complications. First, my mother said the wedding dress pattern I sent her was not the dress she dreamed of for her first daughter's wedding—I had dashed downtown in Palo Alto on the bus during finals to flash through a pattern book at a dime store. But Mother found a pattern to fit the dream: a white taffeta princess-style gown with empire waist, leg-of-mutton sleeves and a sweetheart neckline edged with lace; lace inserts in the skirt were threaded with narrow white velvet ribbon.

The worst complication was the weather, compounding the usually bad road conditions. For days before Christmas, alternating rain and snow made roads to Ramah so impassable that the mail could not be delivered. Getting the groom's parents there became an all-night project. The original plan was to meet their train from Los Angeles in Gallup, but my father telephoned them with new instructions: leave the train west of Gallup at Saunders, in Arizona, where he would meet them and bring them to the ranch via sandy roads through Zuni Pueblo.

My father left in plenty of time to meet them and get back home for spaghetti dinner on Christmas Eve. We held the spaghetti until 8:30 p.m., then decided to eat, even with knots in our tummies, worried about what could have happened. Speculations flew wildly. Maybe there was an emergency with Larry's mother who was diabetic. Maybe the car broke down. We felt sure that my father could not be stuck since he was a survivor of bad roads from years of struggling to remote sheep camps. He always traveled with tire chains, a jack, a shovel and an ax—everything needed to dig out of mudholes and snowdrifts.

By 9 p.m., a rescue party was organized: the groom, my brother Vogtie, the best man Bill Berreyesa, and Paul Davis. Flashlights. Blankets. Shovels. Ax. Tow rope. Wood for fire. Matches. Food and hot coffee. They returned about 4 a.m. My father had met the train on schedule, but on the return through Zuni, he was blocked by cars and trucks already mired in the morass of unprecedented mud and snow. Darkness slowed the digging out.

Larry's mother, whom we called Mother Ruthie, was exhausted but happy to see my birthplace and childhood home she had heard so much about.

WESTERN UNION

1201

R. B. WHITE
PRESIDENT

NEWCOMB CARLTON
CHAIRMAN OF THE BOARD

J. C. WILLEVER
FIRST VICE-PRESIDENT

The filing time shown in the date line on telegrams and day letters is STANDARD TIME at point of origin.   Time of receipt is STANDARD TIME at point of destination

AY5 15 TOUR=B SANBERNARDINO CALIF DEC 28 40 DEC 23 10 30P AM 7 55

EVAN Z VOGT=

CARE GALLUP GAZETTE

ON SANTAFE SCOUT NO 2 ARRIVE MONDAY 455 GALLUP LARRY
ARRIVES BY AUTO MONDAY NOON=
RUTH LOUIS.

Scrap book

2 455.

THE COMPANY WILL APPRECIATE SUGGESTIONS FROM ITS PATRONS CONCERNING ITS SERVICE

A telegram sent by Larry's mother & father - letting us know their arrival times for the wedding

103

Professor Louis Knott Koontz, Larry's stepfather, a history professor at the University of California at Los Angeles, was aghast at this God-forsaken place! (My flashback memories recall his painfully polite Southern manners; for example, he would never ask you to pass the butter. Rather, he would ask you to please help yourself to the butter, assuming that you would take the hint and pass it to him.)

Trying to recall any Christmas gift exchange that wedding year brings a total blank. The day was filled with naps, pressing the dresses, food fixing, and lots of boot scraping and wood fetching for both the fireplace and stove. The wood cookstove had a second important mission: to heat water for dishes and baths. The hot-water pipe to the hot-water tank ran through the firebox of the stove. Baths were scheduled according to water-heating cycles. Running your hand up the tank to see where cold became hot determined how deep a bath was ready, and then there was the debate about who was next. You might assume that the bride and groom would have first dibs, but I remember yielding to my father because of his being cold to the core after working outdoors. The tank in those days was small, but it would handle two baths about a foot deep. None of the luxurious, neck-deep bubble bath you might be visualizing for the bride!

Because of the impassable road from Gallup, the minister with whom we had rehearsed our ceremony could not get to Ramah. The alternate, a minister of the Zuni Christian Reformed Mission, was accustomed to a large church for marriage ceremonies, not a living room, and he hollered the sacred words at our wedding, which was a Christmas candlelight service.

The Gallup minister had been instructed to bring the bridal bouquet, but since he never came, we arranged a charming substitute: three white artificial gardenias from my mother's trunk against a spray of spruce boughs.

Our wedding picture shows us standing beside the Christmas tree against the closed door to the kitchen, over which hangs a flintlock rifle made by one of the Zartman ancestors who was a gunsmith. The rifle above the wedding "altar" is what prompted my Stanford roommate to exclaim when she saw the photo, "Oh, I didn't realize it was a shotgun wedding!"

Instead of leaving immediately for a honeymoon, we attended our wedding dance in the Ramah school gymnasium. The fiddle, guitar and honky-tonk piano music was irresistibly danceable, but we did not stay long, because after I had danced a polka with my old boyfriend, Larry said, "I don't like my bride working up a horse sweat in her lovely dress."

It had already been decided that we should stay at the ranch overnight due to the horrible state of the roads, so the Inn became the honeymoon suite. Years later, while reminiscing about our wedding, I found out that both Vogtie and Jo Ann had slept on the floor in the ranch house in front of the fireplace. Next morning's wake-up call came from my father, calling loudly outside our door (as he did during my childhood), "*Andale*" (come on). If you want to get out of here before the thaw, you better hurry!" So after breakfasting and critiquing the wedding-day happenings, we packed our gifts and tearfully said goodbye to family and guests. We got no further than the bottom of the hill by the corral when Pantalio, a Navajo friend who had been visiting the family, stopped us and handed Larry our traveler's checks that my mother had spotted on the mantel, giving them to Pantalio with instructions to chase us down!

After all this, can you imagine getting stuck in the mud in front of the little cigar-box-size Ramah Post Office? On our way out of town, we stopped to pick up our mail and packages so that Mother—thoroughly exhausted and coming down with the flu—would not have to forward them to us. Fortunately Rudger Lewis, a blessed Ramah old-timer was home and kindly brought a team of horses to pull our car out. It took years for Larry to recover from that embarrassment and humiliation.

Left, my brother, Dr. Evon Z. Vogt Jr., with his wife Naneen. Cambridge, Mass., 1985

Below, Patti & Paul Merrill in their home, Christmas 1977

Left, Jo Ann & Paul Davis at a Davis family reunion in Utah, 1983

The following vignettes of my siblings are gleaned from my files as well as my memory.

Evon Z. Vogt Jr.

Although I recall Vogtie's being a playmate during childhood games of hide-and-seek and kick-the-can, he seemed to grow up and become serious too soon. During my father's absences for sheep business and gold mining, he carried a huge load of responsibility as the man of the ranch—he necessarily became a wood gatherer and fence fixer as well as a cow milker and horse wrangler.

One of his maturing experiences was coping with the Winter of the Big Snow in 1931 when he was 13. He had to supply our home with firewood while my father moved the sheep to a lower elevation in Arizona, hoping to save them. Vogtie said that the only time he ever saw my father break down and cry was on his return home. He explained that the rams were so run down from the trip to Arizona and from hunger that they refused to copulate with the ewes at mating time. He realized that it meant the end of his sheep business.

I recall vividly Vogtie's working in the shearing shed down at Atarque sheep headquarters. He quickly and efficiently tied up each fleece. After it was tied up, it was put in a giant gunnysack, which weighed 100 pounds when full.

I think of the times Vogtie and I rode together in the wagonload of sawdust covering the 100-pound blocks of ice cut from the frozen lake for our icebox. He was very sympathetic when I fell off the wagon and my foot was run over by the back wheel. Because I was wearing boys' work boots, my foot was not crushed.

When he was older, Vogtie worked for the National Park Service as a summer ranger at El Morro National Monument, Bandelier National Monument near Santa Fe and Montezuma National Monument in central Arizona.

With the stimulation of our father's interest in different cultures and the influence of the anthropology books in our library, as well as contact with anthropologists such as Clyde Kluckhohn at the Vogt Ranch, Vogtie decided on anthropology as a career, graduating in 1941 from the University of Chicago. He married Naneen Hiller of Salina, Kan., whom he had met while at the university. Lovingly welcomed by the family, Nan willingly assumed the role of anthropologist's wife with the challenges of strange and varied living conditions and welcoming and feeding all kinds of people while birthing and caring for four children, Shirley Naneen (Skee), Terry, Eric and Charles.

Vogtie completed his doctorate at the University of Chicago and began teaching at Harvard in 1948. He has written many books describing his studies and fieldwork, including the outstanding Harvard Chiapas Project for field research in the Tzotzil-Maya culture. One of his books, *Zinacantan: A Maya Community in the Highlands of Chiapas*, published in 1969 by Belknap Press of Harvard University, won him the Order of the Eagle, Mexico's most prestigious award for foreigners.

As an anthropologist, he brought many interesting colleagues to the ranch, thus changing the breakfast conversation from how many eggs the hens laid yesterday to more intellectual topics. Though Vogtie and I had fewer converging ranch visits because he spent many summers in Chiapas, when he and his family were with us for special family gatherings, I remember the very thoughtful and eloquent toasts he presented for our dinners. I treasure the times Vogtie played his guitar and sang not only many Mexican songs but also old favorites such as "Rancho Grande" and "On Top of Old Smokey."

Jo Ann Vogt

At my father's request to entertain visitors, Jo Ann, age 6, would stand up on a box, with a bright orange scarf tied with a giant side bow around her hair and sing "Let Me Call You Sweetheart." She was always clever at making gifts from whatever—a vase from a peanut butter jar covered with potsherds from our yard.

Both Jo Ann and Patti married men named Paul who were born and grew up in Ramah with the values of this Mormon community, especially the importance of family. When Paul Davis, Jo Ann's husband, returned from World War II, he took over his father's Davis Repair Shop in Ramah, which is where we would interrupt his work to ask that he come and get the Delco started (the Delco motor with its storage batteries was our source of electricity before rural electrification). Paul would come out and perform his magic.

Jo Ann and Paul who have three daughters—Pamela, Krista and Anita—lived in the guesthouse, the Inn, until they built their present home within hollerin' distance of the ranch house. Their home became a hospitality center, welcoming countless relatives, friends and visitors. Evenings would—and still do—often end with a card game or music for both listening and dancing: Jo Ann on violin and Paul on guitar.

Jo Ann became the chief ranch maintenance person after my father's death and when Paul was away, taking pride in being able to climb on the roof with a bucket of tar to repair a leak or stabilizing with concrete the ruin rocks of which the ranch house was built, then replastering them with mud. She would assign teen-agers (and me when I was visiting) tasks such as replacing putty on the old windows.

There was horseback riding, swimming in Ramah Lake and attending Ramah dances with the joyous Western music. Even the ranch chores were more interesting than "sissy" city chores like emptying wastebaskets.

One summer there were thirteen 13-year-olds including family kids and visitors and paying guests. Jo Ann would round up and saddle the horses for guests and arrange turns for the teens to ride to the rodeo. She kept a picnic basket ready to go. And for evening picnics, she would make sure the guitar and violin were in the car for after-dinner music. She initiated many sunrise breakfasts in just the right spot on the mesa for the rising sun to peek through the piñon trees. After these heartwarming summer visits with my children, I would not wash my jeans for several days. Instead, I hung them up and savored the smell of piñon smoke from the campfires!

Jo Ann's tour by car for visitors sometimes included Zuni Pueblo, interesting Indian ruins and the waterfalls above the Ramah Lake. If the bread she was making was not ready to punch down, she would take it along, placing it on the shelf in the back window of the car.

Often referred to as "the little white tornado" because she moves so fast, Jo Ann is known for doing many things all at once: washing clothes, watering strawberries, typing notes and paying bills, cooking for 16, arranging flowers, instructing us to take the manure-spreader and paint rollers back to the storage shed, and sorting unsold rummage junk after the sale.

Patti Vogt

Patti, my youngest sibling, describes herself in an autobiographical sketch in April 2002: "I had an extremely happy childhood, managed to escape the serious household chores, being the youngest, and was left to roam the ranch, discover 'Secret Places' [such as a bower in a grove of junipers where we kept a box of hidden treasure—trinkets discarded by family and friends] in the woods, ride horseback for hours upon the mesa … and spend time in the tree house near the front door, reading everything from *Ivanhoe* to *David Copperfield*." In the description of her childhood, she continues, "I was not completely carefree: I set the table for meals, fed the chickens and dried the dishes —never learned to cook." When the rest of us were away at college, she took over the cow milking. Patti recalls staying at home from school for weeks during a snowstorm. "Home classes were somewhat of a treat, interspersed with games of checkers, Parcheesi, solitaire."

In 1945 during summer vacation from the University of Chicago, she rode horseback to the Ramah Pioneer Day rodeo. On the way home she stopped by the Merrills and visited a few minutes with Paul and Burl Merrill, home on leave from World War II. And quoting her, "That evening after the dance, Paul escorted me home and it was the deciding evening of my life. After that, I could never imagine being married to anyone else."

Fiddle, guitar, and honky-tonk piano dance music to this day still brings me a flood of memories of the Ramah School gymnasium dance hall in the 1930s when entire families came with babies asleep in laundry baskets they placed around the edges of the hall; toddlers dancing with each other; teens self-consciously watching others on the dance floor while they struggle to get it right! The young unmarried men congregated on one side of the hall; the girls, on the opposite side. I'll never forget the heart-pounding suspense when the music started and you watched to see which guy crossing the floor was going to choose you.

After service with the U.S. Marines, Paul returned to New Mexico in 1946 and bought the Fort Wingate Trading Post near the Fort Wingate Army Depot west of Gallup. Patti and Paul married that May. They improved the trading post, which was attached to their home, using the motto, "If we ain't got it, we'll get it." Eventually a separate trading post was built to accommodate the growing business. Special effort was made to maintain the flavor of the old trading post by displaying cowboy sombreros for sale on a rope strung up high across the store, as well as by keeping a stock of metal washtubs and milk buckets and even gingham yardage purchased by Navajo women for their long skirts.

Despite trials and tribulations, Patti and Paul, parents of Judy, Sonya and Scott, always remained calm and fun-loving and welcoming, having proven that Grandma Kate Vogt's life view is very true: life is just overcoming one hardship after another, and the more you overcome, the happier you are!

L to R: Mother, me, Patti & Jo Ann

Memories of Father

As a young man in 1906

At the San Mateo ranch in 1912

Bringing in the Christmas tree, 1930

The first time I saw a grown man cry was at my father's funeral in 1943. This was J.E. Williams, who had worked in about 1938 with my father while he was editor of the *Gallup Gazette*.

Because my father had to put down the buckets of fresh milk and rest when he ran out of breath halfway between the corral and the ranch house, he had a medical checkup in Albuquerque. The doctor told him that his old tuberculosis scar was gone but that he had an enlarged heart with a leaky heart valve and should go on a strict diet and lose at least 20 pounds. Imagine his life without "punkin" pie with whipped cream!

Four days after his medical exam, my father had a heart attack while pushing his pickup through the mud and was taken to the Indian Hospital at Black Rock. Patti, who was living with my husband and me in Los Angeles in order to attend high school there, and I came by train from Los Angeles, and I ache as I recall being greeted with the news that our adored father was gone. The family received an avalanche of letters, telegrams and condolence cards, some from people we had never met—people he had known and helped in some way during his varied career as sheep rancher, scout for gold mines, journalist, National Park Service custodian and self-made anthropologist. Services were held in the First Methodist Church in Gallup. He is buried in Sunset Memorial Park in Albuquerque with a pine tree at the head of his grave.

On Jan. 28, 1943, the following tribute by editor W. A. Barnes was printed in the *Gallup Gazette*.

This section will greatly miss Evon Z. Vogt. His loss is

more than a personal one, although there are few residents of northwestern New Mexico with a wider circle of friends, whose scope included Indians, Spanish-Americans, and many other races, and extended from the most scholarly to the most humble. He will be missed as a friend, and he will also be missed as an enthusiastic and loyal worker for the greater development of this area. Almost from the time of his arrival in New Mexico, then a territory, in 1906, Evon Vogt began delving into its history and archaeology, and developed a remarkably wide acquaintance with prominent students of such matters throughout the country and with men and women of letters who had like tastes. Many of them visited his ranch from time to time, in the course of their field studies. Gallup has cause to remember appreciatively Mr. Vogt's willingness at all times to contribute of his personal time and boundless energies to its upbuilding. He lived a full, unselfish life.

After helping Mother make some decisions about her immediate future, Vogtie and Jo Ann's Paul returned to their wartime assignments, but Jo Ann stayed on with Patti and me to help Mother deal with all the inevitable details following a death. While still at the ranch, I wrote the following letter on Feb. 15, 1943, to my husband Larry, enclosing a twig of juniper.

Isn't this a glorious whiff of woods? I took my first walk on the mesa today with Jo Annie. We had such a lovely time. I wish I had spent every afternoon in like manner during this sad time. The actual reason for the walk was to find the lost cows. A second motive was to examine the planting, erosion-control work and contour furrowing which Daddy had done in accordance with the Soil Conservation Service. They furnished the technical instruction and seed for special erosion-control vegetation; he furnished the labor and materials.

We struck out past The Inn, zigged and zagged to the edge of the mesa overlooking Jose Pino Canyon. The horses were grazing on the winter wheat, but no cows nor any tingling cowbells were in evidence. At the edge we paused to enjoy the glorious view and to reminisce on childhood 'frequentments' of the spot. Jo Annie recalled Paul's kiss at that same spot, which had "made up their minds and hearts" that November.

Soon we were in position to see Shirley Ann's Canyon. At which point we decided to abandon the concern for cows and go visit Jo Ann and Paul's wedding place. The wedding site near the Twin Pines was just as I had visualized, but more intensely beautiful when green following a rainy season. Then—oh sad sight—as we cut away from the edge into the woods, we saw slaughtered junipers and cedars. Some cruel wood hunter had axed out the stumps and left the lovely boughs to die. Then we saw a brush corral, a campsite with several days' campfire ashes and old wagon tracks. And we cussed!

And, oh, there were little soft, melting patches of snow in the shade with crisp lacey edges and a little cold trickle of melted snow running down hill from each. In the paths of these trickles we found luscious new moss—real tender and green, and it reminded us of the days when we walked miles for such moss to transplant as lawns for our playhouse mud homes in the yard. Then we came upon the juniper grove where we buried, during our childhood, a puppy named Gyppy, a chicky named Chicky, and a birdie found dead near the house. We even found the stone marker for "Gyp March 14, 1924" in Vogtie's printing, but no markers for the other two graves.

Back down to Earth—Bang! Refreshed by our nostalgic walk, we now have to get down to business, since tomorrow is the last day at the ranch and we have a million things to do: mothproof the woolens, lock up the tools, arrange for forwarding mail, collect our share of the butchered pig, iron clothes, pack, make a stew to leave for the puppy, instruct Bertha [Navajo friend who was to stay at the ranch] how to start the Delco, etc.

The Navajos are still conferring on a successor for Daddy. They say they want a 'very good friend of Pesoteaje' [Navajos' name for my father—which means "little fat pig," since he was very stout].

Mother visited Jo Ann and Paul in Texas where Paul was stationed before returning to the ranch to "face the music" of how to manage on inadequate income since my father had borrowed so heavily on his life insurance during the Depression. Mother worked at a curio shop in Gallup and then was governess for the children of Edwin Land, inventor of the Polaroid camera, in Santa Fe. But she longed to be home at the ranch.

Mother by her fireplace in 1985 at age 91.
The photo is by Lisa Law.

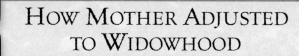
When World War II ended, my sister Jo Ann's husband came home and they built a home in a sunny clearing just back on the mesa from the ranch house, so they were nearby to help Mother.

Eventually it was decided that the family should take advantage of the demand for guest ranch experiences. A formal brochure was printed describing the beauty of the area, availability of interesting sightseeing, home-cooked meals, horseback riding, picnics, overnight camping and sunrise breakfasts on the mesa. To accommodate more guests, a Pueblo-style two-unit guesthouse with shared bath was built to supplement the lodging in the Inn.

So for the next decade or so, paying guests came in the summer, which gave my mother not only income but also abundant challenges as she grappled with menus, kids who were picky eaters and horses hard to find on the mesa for the promised horseback ride. Many guests returned again and again until Jo Ann told one couple who wanted to return, "We are not taking guests because Mother can't see the bugs in the lettuce any more!" As I recall, they insisted they were like family now and would wash the lettuce. And they came.

Mother had her ritual when preparing to leave the ranch house during those winter months she spent away. Set the mousetraps. Tarp the beds under the roof leaks. Put rolled towels against the draft blowing in under the doors. Put the screen in front of the fireplace after stuffing the chimney with crumpled newspaper to keep the "critters" out. Leave propane wall heaters on low to prevent freezing of water pipes. Open door under sink to allow this heat to protect water pipes from freezing.

Clean out the refrigerator. Freeze for later use, or give away leftovers and perishables.

After a month with Vogtie and Nan, a month with me and a month with Patti and Paul, Mother would return to the ranch, take the dead mice from the mousetraps, untarp the beds, check for new roof leaks and seepage through base of her bedroom wall where the melting icicles and snow soaked in, unpack yards of sewing materials and patterns for her planned projects, fill up the wood boxes, and bring the house to life with her cheerful, roaring fires. She once said that it took two weeks of fires to warm up those old ruin rocks of which the ranch house was built.

One of the homemaking skills that Mother perfected was fire building. First she had to procure wood from Trinidad Mares, who had a nearby ranch, or from one of the Navajo neighbors. Cedar was ordered for the cookstove since it makes a quick, hot fire. Piñon was used for the fireplaces because it is slower burning and does not crackle-pop out onto the wood floors and Navajo rugs.

Mother firmly rejected a fireplace grate: "That's stupid to let all those valuable coals drop through the grate where they can't keep the logs burning." At bedtime, the glowing logs were carefully covered with ashes to keep them longer through the night. By morning there were some hot coals to rake out of the ashes and bring to life with the bellows after carefully adding cedar chips or small, pitchy pieces of kindling.

When starting a fire from scratch, the secret was lots of crumpled paper, a handful of cedar chips, several very small (pitchy if available) pieces of kindling, then adding heavy logs once the fire was well-established.

Filling the wood boxes was one of the kids' chores. We learned to stack a huge load across the extended arms instead of just hugging a few pieces like a babe in arms. We sometimes used the wheelbarrow when it was around. There was always a designated piling place outside for the ashes, safely away from trees and bushes since some of the ashes could have glowing embers. Here is a delightful quote from Mother when she explained to me on the phone why she had a pain in her ribs from a fall while carrying a bucket of ashes: "I was just walkin' along, singing a little song and tripped and fell!"

After our wedding in 1940, Larry and I returned to Stanford University, rented a charming little guesthouse in Palo Alto where we lived until our graduation in 1942. Larry's first professional job was with the Aluminum Company of America in Los Angeles. In January of 1943 the sorrow and shock of my father's death was somewhat alleviated by my news of expecting the first Vogt grandchild. Alan Robert was born Sept. 4, 1943, in Culver City, Calif.

Aluminum Company of America transferred Larry to its Phoenix plant, so we chugged off across the desert in our Model A Ford with boiling radiator. At the end of World War II we returned to Los Angeles to a consulting job, then back to Stanford where Larry taught returning GIs who wanted engineering degrees. Our second child, Bruce Gregory, was born in Palo Alto on Sept. 4, 1949.

In 1954 a manufacturing partnership venture took us to Los Angeles again. It was a blessing to be near Larry's mother Ruthie for her last days. She died not long after the birth of our daughter Catherine on Sept. 29, 1955.

During all those years I nearly always returned to the Vogt Ranch with the children during their summer vacations, to bask in the loving welcome of my family, to enjoy the nieces and nephews, to hike on the mesa and picnic up the canyons.

Our next move was to New York City, where Larry worked in engineering education for the General Electric Company. It was hard to say goodbye to friends and home in Palo Alto after 20 years. We bravely sorted the accumulation of clothes, household equipment, tools, toys, science fair displays, unfinished sewing projects, etc. Here is my poem that described it all.

THINGS YOU CAN HAVE FOR
YOUR VERY OWN

(On sorting to move to New York -1963)

One-half a crinkled wrinkled old pajama
   string,
Less than half a lovingly pressed butterfly
   wing,
A carefully kept box full of elastic without
   zing,
Some ancient college choruses requiring
   courage to sing,
All kinds of special feathers that my Cub
   Scouts used to bring,
And a rusty lemon squeezer where the seeds
   still cling,
A dusty bunch of pine cones that I guess
   I'd better fling,
Reams and reams of recipes I clipped for
   some whing-ding,
A fluffy, floppy rabbit full of memories that
   sting,
A never-once-worn hat that I purchased
   once in Spring,
A spaghetti-tangle of ribbons that would
   match most anything,
A dinky dab of purple beads who'd bother
   to restring,
Parts of teeny-tiny motors that once ran
   without a ping,
And at least four decks of cards missing ace
   or eight or King.
If these aren't what you're most longing for,
   why then I say,"By jing,
On the day of our departing take our bath
   tub's dirty ring!"

Although the distance from our New York home to
the ranch was greater, we still returned for summer visits.

Thirty years of joys and sorrows during our marriage finally led to the following announcement by
Larry and me in 1970:

    Just as Pooh Bear
    Patiently here on his branch
    Has grown to understand
    And not be sad,

So, too, will you accept our news:
Barby and Larry are separated.
not by cracker crumbs in bed;
not by toothpaste squoze in the middle;
not by women's liberation.
Just a gradual, final realization that
New paths for each is best now.
It is without bitterness.
It is just with acceptance
Of the suchness of life.

In 1971 I moved with my daughter Cathy to New Mexico to be near my family at the Vogt Ranch. We settled in Albuquerque where I worked at the University of New Mexico School of Medicine. One day when I went to visit my niece Kristi's in-laws, Dovie and Jim Mallery, I was introduced to Jim's brother Richard, who was visiting. We discovered that we were kindred spirits, both fascinated with words and all kinds of people. Richard was an English professor, retired from New York University. After his wife Ruth's death, he courageously completed two more years of teaching, then retired and moved to Santa Fe where he lived in a cozy guesthouse. We fell in love during a courtship that included his writing me many love poems—which he playfully sent air mail to Albuquerque, 50 miles away, "because they were so important!" After my divorce from Larry, we married in 1974, I resigned my job at UNM, and we bought a Pueblo-style home in Santa Fe.

We cherished our time together, getting acquainted with each other's friends and family, sharing our life histories. We treasured our frequent trips to the Vogt Ranch where my mother was still baking and sewing and gardening and enjoying the "comings and goings" of her extended family at age 83 in spite of heart trouble and cataract operations.

Precious memories of our beautiful years together have comforted me ever since Richard's death in 1978.

My children: Cathy, 3 - Alan, 15 & Bruce, 9,
taken in 1958

For my children, Alan, Bruce and Cathy, summer vacation visits to the Vogt Ranch were joyful and learning times.

Alan, born in 1943, was Grandma Shirley's first grandchild and his sayings were much quoted. When he was only 3, upon his arrival at the ranch, he commented about all the signs he saw along the highway. When asked what they said, his answer was, "Nothing. Signs don't have mouths." While attending a Ramah dance, he watched intently the fiddler keeping time with his foot. Alan whispered to me, "Does that man have a motor in his leg?"

One of my favorite memories of Alan at the ranch is his running around the yard with a chicken feather in each hand. He often lovingly presented me with a handful of sow bugs—the ones that roll into a ball when touched. His love of nature probably originated with walks on the mesa when I taught him to identify the various evergreens by examining the needles. If the needle is flat, it's fir; if square, a spruce. If needles are in pairs, it's a piñon; if in a bundle, a pine. In later years, when he was a nature counselor at a summer camp in Northern California, he taught many little campers how to identify all the cone-bearing trees.

Bruce was born on Alan's sixth birthday in 1949. His real kindred spirit among the cousins was Jo Ann's daughter Kristi, with whom he once built a Pueblo-style horno (oven) like the ones he'd seen in Zuni. Using rocks to form the dome, they then mudded them over. With permission, they built a fire inside and closed the opening with a huge flagstone. Jo Ann gave them a hunk of bread dough from her baking batch, and after shaping it round like the traditional Pueblo loaf, they baked it in the oven.

Bruce was a capable chore boy. He filled the wood boxes by the kitchen stove and by the fireplace. He especially enjoyed fire building and showed Grandma how to make a longer-lasting newspaper wad for starting the kindling: he rolled a single sheet of newspaper and tied it in a simple knot.

Jo Ann's three girls looked forward to little Cathy's visit so they could use her as their fashion model. They creatively dressed her from the fantastic collection of old costumes in Grandma's trunk. I vividly remember the Balinese dancer with brightly colored silk scarves on her head and wrists and ankles and a jewel in her navel!

Cathy's chores were simple ones like tucking the ripening strawberries under the leaves of the plant to hide them from the birds. Or sitting on the grass in the enclosed garden next to the ranch house, shucking corn on the cob for supper. Or picking up chips from the woodpile for fire starting.

The children could wander freely on the mesa, away from traffic or strangers, exploring rocky crevices, collecting lichen-covered rocks and seedpods and the enchanting little twiggy things in the various stages of new growth—some of them so lacey and dainty they could have been from a fairy garden. They could be called home by clanging on the old Ford rim, which hung on bailing wire under the kitchen porch roof.

Following a family gathering in September 2000 during which we were reminiscing about my parents, my niece Nita mailed me a precious packet: a collection of handwritten messages from my mother and my father to the Ramah Trading Company. The messages are written with scratchy fountain pen or pencil on snippets of torn paper, on old letterhead, and on backs of used envelopes bearing two-cent stamps and dated 1919 and 1920! Since my parents did not yet own a car (they traveled by wagon or horseback in 1919 and 1920), they were sending for supplies and their mail via various neighbors and/or sheep-camp employees.

There are 57 pieces in the collection, which was given to my niece by Grace Bond, widow of the last trader to do business in the old cut-stone building, the Ramah Trading Post, constructed in 1902 by Giles and Robert Master of England. Grace found the messages in an accumulation of time-weathered documents in a storage area near the attic while cleaning out the old store to sell it. Her gift will be appreciated forever.

The Ramah Trading Company was the general mercantile as well as the post office and had the only telephone in town on which telegrams could be received and sent. It also had a huge, potbellied stove around which customers gathered to warm up and catch up on the news.

The traders bought wool, lambs, and piñons from the Native Americans of the area, who could buy most of the things they needed from the trading post, stocked with an amazing array of goods, as shown by this list, compiled from all the messages: seven-day coffee, matches, cartridges, yeast, barbed wire, half soles and shoe tacks, oats and corn for stock, nails, ink, flour, lard, canned goods, salt, sugar, flour, cough syrup, gasoline, coal oil, quilts, film, tobacco and tobacco papers, hay, sox, shoes, overshoes, overalls, cocoa, soap, sorghum, sarsaparilla, red chile, nuts, and a lamp chimney. Not mentioned in any of the notes are other things that I remember: yard goods, buckets, rope, meats, sewing needles and thread, and tools.

All but a few of the notes start with "please give the bearer . . ." and in addition to listing needed supplies requested that the bearer be given credit to make purchases that were to be charged to E.Z. Vogt. On the back of one of the messages is a penciled list of charges that totaled $900.22. No doubt payment was awaiting shearing season and the sale of wool.

A note from my mother reads, "Please give Narcisso [a neighbor] some medicine for his horse and the mail." And another: "Please give bearer two sacks of herders' flour and a bottle of cough syrup. Also a bottle of medicine which he wants. I cannot understand what it is."

From E. Z. Vogt: "Please give bearer 8 rolls black barb wire—the heavy kind—one lamp chimney No.2. plain, 10 lbs. potatoes, 2 35 lb. sacks second grade flour, 4 lbs. coffee ground, 2 cans baking powder K. C. and oblige. I'll be up later this afternoon. Please give the boy 1 pair overalls."

Dick White was one of the traders who succeeded the Master Brothers. The following message reflects my father's tremendous trust of Dick and their friendship: "Dick: Be sure to get this letter off. If sack is closed just lay it on top of sack so it will go, as it is important. EZV." Another note: "Dear Dick: In case I should have a telegram from Mr. Carr in the next few days which needs reply, will you please answer for me. I am going to Quemado and will be back Wednesday. Con el favor de Dios. Just hold our mail until we return and oblige. EZV."

The following note from my mother, apparently after my father had gone back to sheep camp, says: "Dear Mr. White: Would you please send this note over to Nettie for me, as I am not feeling well and would like to have her come out and help me. Very truly, Mrs. Vogt." Nettie, a sister of Paul Davis, was Mother's occasional helper.

One of the longest lists is the following, undoubtedly items needed for my father's sheep camps in the nearby Zuni Mountains:

8 bales of alfalfa

1 sack corn or oats

1/2 dozen BBA shears (no other)

20 wool sox

1 bottle coal oil (1 pint)

50 cent chewing tobacco

25 cent Toro tob. papers

6 red bandanas

1 box 5/8 shoe tax

1 box matches

1 white hat size 7

2 cans Kemp's Branding Paint (I don't want any but Kemp's. If you haven't got it would you please order it over the phone at once. I have got to have it by 25th. Cotton's have it.)

200 lbs. flour

Send bill for above supplies & oblige. E Z Vogt.

In a note to Mr. Kelsey, a trader who succeeded Mr. White, the request is for black board paint for the Tinaja School, which is near El Morro.

I treasure the memory of all the Navajos gathered at the store—their horses tied under the Lombardy poplar trees along the irrigation ditch across the street from the trading post. Some sat on the loading dock in colorful native dress, eating canned tomatoes out of the can, or stood around the potbellied stove in the store warming themselves.

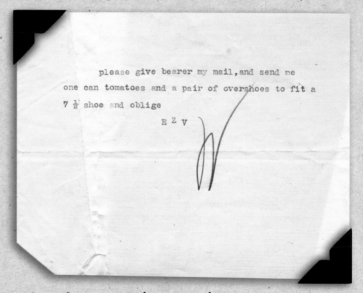

please give bearer my mail, and send me one can tomatoes and a pair of overshoes to fit a 7 ½ shoe and oblige

E Z V

A message from my father requesting supplies be sent from the Ramah Trading Post

Wheelwright Museum of the American Indian, Santa Fe, NM.

Mother & Father on their honeymoon - dangling their bare feet in the Upper Pecos river, July 1915

Mother sawing an ice block from the pond near the Vogt Ranch, a Navajo neighbor helping with the tongs, 1920

Mother in 1914

After she stopped running the "dude" ranch, my mother had many peaceful, happy years, enjoying her homemaking and gardening, family picnics and campouts. When she became 80, she announced assertively that she was not going to sleep in a sleeping bag any more, and furthermore she changed my father's rules about having to be fully dressed for breakfast! She often ate in her robe and dressed later when she knew what clothes would be appropriate for the planned activities of the day.

Mother enjoyed reading and was delighted with the advent of the large-print books. She especially liked Mary Roberts Rinehart. She also started knitting, which she could not fit into her busy days in earlier years. Asked for whom she was knitting the sweater, she answered, "For whomever it fits if I ever finish it!"

Horseback riding was a longtime pleasure, from her honeymoon through the years to when she rode with paying guests. She knew many trails back on the mesa and up the canyon.

Mother thought weather predictions were ridiculous. She believed that weather is part of life; you just cope with whatever comes. The fairyland scenes resulting from snow that fell silently during the night were a delight to her and to me. We often talked on the phone after a heavy snow, trying to decide whose trees were more beautiful. She was a skilled driver who seemed almost to enjoy the challenge of a snow-laden road. During the winter of 1931 her legs got frostbitten while she was shoveling snowdrifts off the road to Ramah. She had gone to give us a ride home from school because she did not want us to walk in the storm.

During Mother's last years, she had supper each evening with Jo Ann and Paul, who live a short distance through the piñon trees from the ranch house. Jo Ann thoughtfully included her on trips to Gallup, thus offering companionship as well as giving Mother a chance to do her own errands. Patti and Paul were also in constant contact. When there was discussion about discontinuing fireplace wood because of the expense, Paul said, "As long as she is able to build a fire, I will supply her with firewood."

There were daily trips to the Ramah Post Office. One day when I was with her, a friend from near El Morro came up to chat. After Mother explained how she was dealing with decisions involving the family, the friend commented, "I guess you got some say-so, ain't cha!"

Family members included Mother in special trips—to Hawaii, New Orleans and even on a Caribbean cruise—and there were many trips to visit friends and relatives. Her last little journey was to see the family of Vogtie's daughter Skee Teleki in Canada. A happy, smiling photo of mother was taken at the Teleki Farm just 11 days before we all gathered to say farewell to her. She died on June 11, 1986. She apparently had a stroke while reaching for her ringing telephone. I was calling from San Francisco to tell her of the birth of her great-granddaughter Danica Rain Ivanovich.

A touching service was held at the Mormon Church in Ramah, and Mother was buried beside my father in Albuquerque. If we had not been crying so hard, we might have been chuckling about her remark to Paul 10 years before while watching him in his workshop in Fort Wingate: "I love the smell of that cedar. I hope you are going to make me a coffin of it." So he did, and Patti lined it with deep-rose-colored satin. It had black wrought iron hinges and latch. Paul stored it in the rafters of his barn for 10 years. Aunt Kay was the only one who asked why she was buried in her stocking feet. The coffin was a wee bit too short, so her shoes had to be left off! It was an elegant coffin and seemed so appropriate for this beloved lady with a lifetime of enjoying the smells and sights and feel of things around her.

Following are quotations from Mother's memorial service on June 16, 1986.

Shirley will always remain in my heart. Shirley left a family of growers and sewers and painters and guitar players and pastry makers and movers and shakers, who will continue in Shirley's hospitable way to fill our lives with love and happiness.

–By William Stripp, husband of granddaughter Pamela

Her special qualities of cheerfulness, thoughtfulness of others, courage, calmness in crises, patience, optimism, appreciation of others for all that they did for her, and her amazing acceptance of the changes over the years will be remembered forever.

–From eulogy read by Paul Davis

Mother sweeping snow from the portal of the original ranch house built of rocks from ruins on the property. Note the stove pipe over the kitchen at left, 1915.

Me, at age 1, outside the sheep camp tent with campfire smudges on my face, 1921

aying goodbye to my book is a little sad. No more adventures into the past as I browse through family files. No more excuses for not accepting more requests to volunteer for this and that, though one of those I did accept involved telling about my childhood and reading excerpts from this book.

At two Elderhostels I was among seniors who shared life stories, listened and laughed and cried and sang and hiked and visualized and meditated. My writing has also been interrupted from time to time by my own physical challenges, home and yard maintenance projects, visits from family and friends and occasional ennui!

For 14 years I have been turning the pages of my mind in search of memories of my life from childhood days forward. Into my writing I have woven information from my father's copious files. These

files from my father include a folder marked "For the Book I Plan to Write." I have used some of the stories from that folder.

Now I close with these special memories of the times my father took me with him to sheep camp, bouncing along in an old pickup over sagebrush and arroyos while he was singing one of his three favorite songs: "Let Me Call You Sweetheart," "Paloma Blanca,"(White Dove) or "Que Bueno Es Pan con Queso a la Revuelta al Rancho" (How Good Is Bread With Cheese Upon My Return to the Ranch)—a well-known song in the Southwest.

My mother's love of homemaking and joy of being at home was emphatically demonstrated one summer day in 1985 after she had been visiting me in Santa Fe. When her telephone seemed disconnected, she walked up to the casita to ask if the phone there was working. Yes. So she started up her old 1964 Ford and drove up to Jo Ann's to use her phone to report the trouble to the telephone company. She then sorted overripe apricots from a huge pan full of them and made jam. She fixed our lunch and washed the dishes, refilled the hummingbird feeder, watered her flower garden, swatted flies and baked cookies. Then she sorted all the accumulated mail, browsed through and discarded a bunch of clothing catalogs. Such energy at age 91!

You probably have been wondering all through the book when I was going to explain the importance of bailing wire in ranch life. Some of you may not know that bailing wire was used in the old days to hold together bales of hay. If it was not folded and tied with a twist of the end when you cut it off the hay, you were likely to find a spaghetti-tangle of wires on the barn floor!

Bailing wire was used to fix gates, fences, cars, windmills, wire mattress springs, whatever. It was sometimes used as a cotter pin to hold the wheels of a little red wagon, to unlock a car without a key, and even to make a picker-upper of a valuable that fell through a knothole in the ranch's wood-plank floor. As mentioned before, for 70 years it has been used to hang the old Ford brake drum under the kitchen porch roof at the ranch—our dinner bell.

I am intensely appreciative of my peaceful childhood at the Vogt Ranch. I wish more children would enjoy watching ants build their homes. I realize that my parents' calmness and determination in dealing with their problems gives me the strength to cope. I realize too, that my parents' lifestyle of hard work combined with play helps me remember to take time out for fun.

Daily I count my blessings; a loving, helping family and caring, sharing friends and the ability at age 83 to maintain my home and myself. I am able to create some beauty around me and contribute in small ways to the care of our earth and the well-being of my community and to sustain a dream of peace for all.

And I am grateful that my father's wish came true, that he found "a girl who could fit in here and be contented with the sky and plain, the timbered ridges, red mesas and wonderful mountains. One who could ride with me and be happy in the Great Solitude."

ABOUT THE AUTHOR

*Me as I look today,
by Nancy Dahl, 2003*

Barbara Vogt Mallery was home-birthed in 1920 at the Vogt Ranch in northwestern New Mexico. She attended school in nearby Ramah, finished high school in Palo Alto, Calif. and graduated from Stanford University in 1941. Barbara married classmate Lawrence Bell in 1940. They lived in Palo Alto and in Southern California and in Scotia, NY. Barbara enjoyed the challenge of describing in letters her adventures as mother of three, helpmate to an engineer working in industry and teaching at Stanford.

After 30 years of joys and sorrows, Barbara and Larry divorced in 1971 and Barbara moved to New Mexico to be near her family at the Vogt Ranch. She later married Richard Mallery, a professor emeritus of New York University who died in 1978. Barbara worked for the New Mexico Health and Environment Department and for St. John's College in Santa Fe. She lives in Santa Fe, NM.